THE KURDS:
my friends in the north

The Kurds - my friends in the north

Published by The Conrad Press in the United Kingdom 2021

Tel: +44(0)1227 472 874
www.theconradpress.com
info@theconradpress.com

ISBN 978-1-913567-79-8

Typesetting and Cover Design by: Charlotte Mouncey, www.bookstyle.co.uk

The Conrad Press logo was designed by Maria Priestley.

THE KURDS:
my friends in the north

A story of broken dreams,
bloodshed and betrayal

JOHN COOKSON

For my parents Geoffrey and Nancy Cookson

Contents

Foreword

In October 2019 former US President Donald Trump defied international criticism and withdrew American support for Kurdish allies battling the jihadists of Islamic State in Syria. The Kurds had spearheaded the destruction of I.S's so-called caliphate and had suffered thousands of casualties on the battlefield - so Trump's action amounted to a huge betrayal. I'd always planned to write a book about the Kurds; Trump forced my hand. The time was right.

Whilst I hope my research stands up to academic scrutiny, what follows is not a scholarly tome for egg-heads; it's more an impulsive and hopefully illuminating insight into a people who've always shown me kindness and respect as I went about my journalistic business of chronicling their lives and their eternal quest for independence.

Although I retain a huge affection for the indomitable Kurds, I've remained true to the journalistic principle of objectivity, so there will be anecdotes and comments which might appear mean-spirited and disapproving to some Kurdish friends.

But the reality is I've attended meetings when Kurdish ministers have brazenly demanded kickbacks on multimillion-dollar contracts and I've spent time with Kurdish militia who didn't always play by the internationally accepted rules of war.

Warts and all is the only way I can write, and for those who feel hurt by some revelations I'd say: soak it up and accept the overall tone of this book as being a generous tribute to a remarkable race of people who've suffered so much at the hands of invaders throughout the millennia.

KURDISH CHRONOLOGY - THE LAST 100 YEARS

1920: Kurds are promised their own land under the Treaty of Sèvres, one of the treaties that ends the First World War and dismantles the Ottoman empire. But the pledge made by Britain, France and the US to the Kurds goes unfulfilled, and national borders are drawn across the hoped-for region of Greater Kurdistan.

Kurdish nationalism grows, and the rest of the century will be marked by revolts and uprisings by Kurdish tribal leaders against the nation states that oppose their demand for self-rule and try to suppress Kurdish identity.

1923: The Turkish Republic is founded by Mustafa Kemal Ataturk after a war of independence, with a Turkish-centric, centralised state that faces uprisings from Kurdish tribes. These are quashed with military force. Later, policies repressing Kurdish rights and identity are put in place, with Kurdish languages banned and Kurds forced to 'Turkify' their names, as well as the names of towns and villages.

1946: The Soviet Union, which occupies Iran alongside the Allies and is trying to annex the country's north-west, encourages Kurdish nationalism and the establishment of a self-ruling mini-state that claims autonomy from Iran called the Republic of Mahabad. The short lived republic is destroyed when the Soviets pull out

1958: Tribal leader Mustapha Al-Barzani, who had fought for the Mahabad Republic, returns to his homeland in northern

Iraq to lead an uprising for an autonomous Kurdish nation. This starts a war against the Iraqi state that lasts until 1970.

1962: A fifth of Syrian Kurds in the largely Kurdish northeast region are stripped of Syrian nationality, barring them from employment, education, civil property rights and political representation. Many lose their land, which the state hands to Arab and Assyrian settlers.

1972: Iran's Shah asks Richard Nixon, US president, to help him support Barzani's uprising against the Iraqi state. Iraq is Soviet-aligned, and Nixon agrees to begin supplying the Kurds with weapons. In 1975, however, the Shah makes a deal with Iraq, cutting out the Kurds and causing their abandonment by the Americans.

1978: The Kurdistan Workers' party (PKK), a radical militant group, is founded by Abdullah Ocalan, a Turkish Kurd, with the aim of toppling the Turkish government using violent means.

1984: The PKK uses Kurdish northern Iraq as a base for a guerrilla war against Turkey, which continues on and off for the next four decades. The PKK commits terrorist atrocities, while Turkey arrests and imprisons politically active Kurds.

1987 to 1988: In the closing days of the Iran-Iraq war, Saddam Hussein, the Ba'athist dictator, launches a genocidal campaign against Iraqi Kurds, culminating in a chemical attack on the Kurdish town of Halabja. It kills up to 5,000 people in a single day.

1991: A Kurdish uprising in northern Iraq is encouraged by the administration of George H.W. Bush, US president, after Saddam was pushed out of Kuwait in the first Gulf war. It is crushed by the Iraqi dictator. Hundreds of thousands of Kurds flee into the mountain ranges on the Iraqi-Turkish border. The devastation prompts the US and other western partners to create a no-fly zone to stop Saddam from bombing the Kurds. It remains in place until the US-led invasion of 2003.

2003: The US works with Iraqi Kurds and the Kurdistan region during the invasion of Iraq. After the fall of Saddam, the Kurdistan Region of Iraq gains autonomous status and enjoys an economic boom.

2011: The Syrian civil war presents an opportunity for Syrian Kurds to form an autonomous administration in north-east Syria. The US chooses experienced Kurdish fighters of the PKK-aligned People's Protection Units (YPG) to spearhead the fight in north-east Syria against ISIS, extreme Sunni jihadis who have taken advantage of the power vacuum to seize control of a vast territory across Syria and Iraq.

2015: The collapse of a faltering peace process between the PKK and the Turkish state leads to a surge in violence. Urban warfare erupts in cities across Turkey's Kurdish majority south-east and a wave of PKK-linked bombings hit cities to the west, including the capital Ankara and Istanbul.

The breakdown in the talks, that had been spearheaded by Turkish President Recep Tayyip Erdogan and accompanied by reforms aimed at improving Kurdish rights, is followed by a wave of arrests of Kurdish activists and politicians.

2018: In December, Trump makes his first threat to withdraw US troops from the fight against ISIS, saying the jihadis have been defeated. He moderates his position to a partial drawdown after a furious backlash in the US and abroad at the abandoning of the Kurds who have been allies of the US in combating the extremists in north-east Syria.

2019: The Syrian Democratic Forces - made up of Kurdish fighters as well as Arab groups opposed to President Bashar Al-Assad's regime - finally win territorial victory over ISIS in north-east Syria with backing from an international coalition led by the US.

October 7 2019: Trump says US troops are leaving the Turkish-Syrian border area, where they have been conducting joint patrols with Turkey as part of a mechanism to reassure Ankara that separatist Kurdish fighters will not use the area to attack Turkey. Trump is widely seen as giving a green light to a long-threatened Turkish military advance into this territory, pitting America's Kurdish allies against an enemy they consider a greater threat than ISIS.

WHERE ARE THE KURDS?

Getting hold of accurate figures for current Kurdish populations in 2021 is hard-going because recent conflicts have created so much displacement and the numbers have sometimes been manipulated by Kurds themselves and national governments, for political ends.

According to America's Central Intelligence Agency's

Factbook: Kurds in Turkey form almost twenty percent of the population, although Kurdish sources maintain its twenty five percent or around twenty million people.

Kurds in Iraq are the largest ethnic group numbering just over six million or around twenty per cent of the population.

In Iran, Kurds live mostly in the north-west and the north-east of the Islamic Republic. Numbering around seven million, they make up around eight percent of the population.

Many tens of thousands of Kurds have fled northern Syria in recent years, but before the civil war there were 1.6 million Kurdish people, or nine percent of the population, that nation's largest ethnic group.

The Kurdish diaspora is around 1.5 million with pockets of Kurdish communities across the globe.

Before the Lebanese civil war in the 1980s and Israel's invasion and occupation, there were around 100,000 Kurds in Lebanon, mainly in urban areas like including the slums of Beirut, or in Tripoli, Sidon and Tyre.

That figure has dropped to around 60,000 now, with many Kurds unable to acquire citizenship; some are even registered as Palestinian or their status: *'qaid al-dars'* or under consideration.

There were no formally recognised Kurdish territories in the former Soviet Union but it's estimated, very roughly, there are about half a million Kurds mainly in the Caucuses with approximately 200,000 in Azerbaijan, 75,000 in Armenia and 40,000 in Georgia.

Other large Kurdish communities now in modern day Russia include 35,000 in Siberia with 30,000 of them settled in Vladivostok.

Successive periods of political and social turmoil from the 1960s onwards forced around 1.3 million Kurds to find sanctuary in Western Europe. Most have settled in Germany, Austria, the Benelux countries, France, Switzerland and the United Kingdom where there's a thriving Kurdish community in parts of north London and former mill towns of Yorkshire, like Dewsbury. In the UK's 2011 Census, 50,000 people gave their ethnicity as Kurdish.

Canada is another destination for Kurds, mainly political refugees or those seeking better economic prospects. Latest figures from Statistics Canada put the Kurdish population at almost 12,000.

In the United States Kurds from Iraq and Iran started to arrive in significant numbers into Nashville, Tennessee in 1976. The south of the city is now home to the largest US Kurdish community and is nicknamed Little Kurdistan, a neighbourhood clustered around the Salahadeen Centre, the first Kurdish mosque to open in North America.

As of the time of writing the Nashville Police Department employed one Kurdish police officer and was training another, which might be useful in combatting the worrying trend of the present generation of US born Kurds joining street gangs.

Reliable sources estimate there are 20,000 ethnic Kurds in the US.

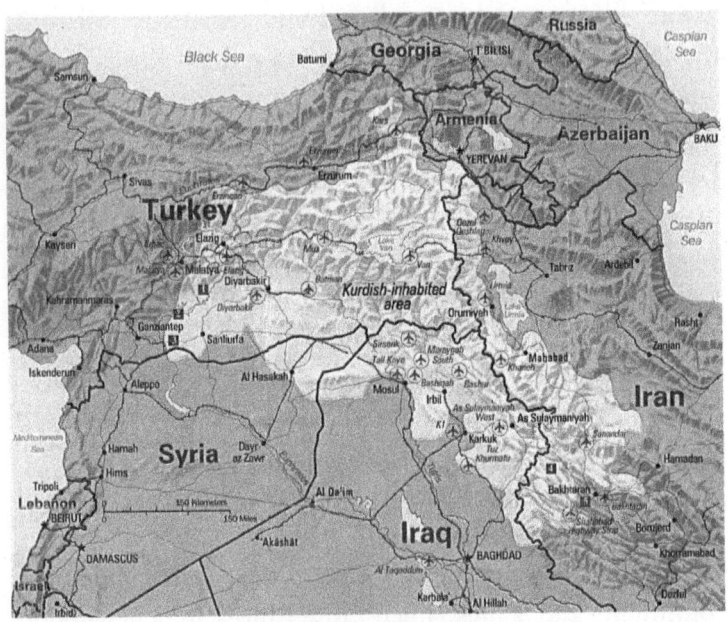

Map of Kurdish region

GIRLS OF MANY LANDS

No. 30.   A Series of 50

KURDISTAN

The Kurds are a very wild and freedom-loving nomadic race. Some of them live in tents, though others will camp out on their pastures in the summer and live in villages in the winter.

The women share the life of the men but are allowed considerable freedom, and they go about with faces unveiled.

Issued by

MAJOR DRAPKIN & Co.

(Branch of United Kingdom Tobacco Co. (1929), Ltd.)

London.

Cigarette card 1929

KURDISH POLITICAL GROUPS IN THE MIDDLE EAST.

IRAQ:

Action Party for the Independence of Kurdistan
Democratic Patriotic Alliance of Kurdistan
Gorran Movement
Islamic Fayli Grouping in Iraq
Islamic Group Kurdistan
Islamic Kurdish Society
Islamic Movement of Kurdistan
Islamic Kurdish League
Kurdish Revolutionary Hezbollah
Kurdish Tribal Association
Kurdistan Communist Party
Kurdistan Democratic Party (KDP)
Kurdistan Islamic Union
Kurdistan Toilers' Party
Kurdish Socialist Party
Kurdistan Conservative Party
Kurdistan National Democratic Union
Kurdistan Socialist Democratic Party
Kurdistan Revolutionary Party
Patriotic Union of Kurdistan (PUK)

IRAN:

Kurdistan Democratic Party of Iran (KDPI)
Kurdistan Free Life Party (PJAK)
Eastern Kurdistan Units (YRK)
Women's Defence Forces (HPJ)

Komola
Kurdish United Front
Kurdistan Freedom Party (PAK)

TURKEY:
Communist Party of Kurdistan (KKP)
Democracy Party (DEP)
Democratic People's Party (DEHAP)
Democratic Society Party (DTP)
Hereketa İslamiya Kurdistan (HİK)
Kurdish Hizbollah
Islamic Party of Kurdistan (PİK)
Kurdistan Communities Union (KCK)
Kurdistan Democratic Party/North (KDP/Bakur)
Kurdistan Workers' Party (PKK)
People's Defence Forces (HPG)
National Liberation Front of Kurdistan (ERNK)
Peace and Democracy Party (BDP)
Democratic Regions Party (DBP)
Peoples' Democratic Party (HDP)
People's Democracy Party (HADEP)
People's Labour Party (HEP)
Revolutionary Party of Kurdistan (PŞK)
Rights and Freedoms Party (HAK-PAR)
Society for the Rise of Kurdistan
Xoybûn (CSK)
Workers Vanguard Party of Kurdistan (PPKK)
Kurdistan Freedom Hawks (TAK)
Marxist–Leninist Communist Party (MLKP)
DHKP/C

Communist Party of Turkey/Marxist–Leninist (TKP/ML)
Revolutionary Headquarter
Communist Labour Party of Turkey/Leninist (TKEP/L)
Patriotic Revolutionary Youth Movement (YDG-H)
Civil Protection Units (YPS)
Civil Protection Units-Women (YPS-Jin)

SYRIA:
Kurdish National Alliance in Syria (HNKS)
Syrian Democratic Council (SDC)
Democratic Union Party (Syria) (PYD)
Movement for a Democratic Society (TEV-DEM)
People's Protection Units (YPG)
Women's Protection Units (YPJ)
Asayish
Kurdish National Council (ENKS)
Kurdistan Democratic Party of Syria (KDP-S)
Kurdish Supreme Committee
Kurdish Democratic Political Union
Euphrates Volcano
Jabhat al-Akrad
United Freedom Forces

KURDISH NATIONAL ANTHEM

Oh, enemy! The Kurdish people live on,
They have not been crushed by the weapons of any time
Let no one say Kurds are dead, they are living
They live and never shall we lower our flag

We are descendants of the red banner of the revolution
Look at our past, how bloody it is
Let no one say Kurds are dead, they are living
They live and never shall we lower our flag

The Kurdish youth rise bravely,
With their blood they coloured the crown of life
Let no one say Kurds are dead, they are living
They live and never shall we lower our flag

We are the descendants of the Medes and Cyaxares
Kurdistan is our religion, our credo,
Let no one say Kurds are dead, they are living
They live and never shall we lower our flag

The Kurdish youth are ready and prepared,
To give their life as the supreme sacrifice
Let no one say Kurds are dead, they are living
They live and never shall we lower our flag

1. Magic carpet ride

Dusk on a dirt road in lawless east Turkey and another chapter in the world of television news gathering was unfolding. The year was 1993 and cameraman Tim and I were on assignment during the dog days of a Turkish summer. We'd found ourselves outside the curiously named city of Batman which my guidebook described as: 'a sprawl of non-descript cement buildings of no historical interest - charmless'.

I wouldn't disagree.

We'd been dispatched to east Turkey by Sky News to cover the story of a British engineer David Rowbottom and his Australian travelling companion and cousin, Tanya Miller, who'd been snatched at gunpoint by Kurdish separatists known as the PKK.

The hapless pair, both twenty-eight, were captured after they'd set off from the town of Tatvan on mountain bikes to explore a nearby extinct volcano.

I didn't have a lot of sympathy.

Hadn't they known it was dangerous to take an afternoon cycle ride in a region where at least twenty five people were being killed every day in battles between the Turkish Army and the PKK?

The kidnapping was a big story in the UK and, as we'd already been in Turkey for two days, I knew my foreign editor Nick Jennings would be impatiently tapping his fingers in London waiting for a Cookson 'exclusive,' namely: an interview with the kidnapped pair held at gunpoint somewhere in the Taurus Mountains.

Turkish secret police had tailed us since we'd flown in to Diyarbakir, near the border with Iraq, but we'd given the spooks the slip and arranged a clandestine rendezvous with two PKK fighters outside Batman.

They'd agreed to smuggle us to their hideout where Rowbottom and Miller were being held.

When we met the two PKK fighters had already unfurled two carpets next to their truck.

'Mr John and Mr Tim, lay down on the carpets, we're going to roll you up in them and take you up the mountain in the back of our truck,' grunted Harjar, guerrilla number one.

It sounds like madness, dear reader, but we journalists live in a world of sudden, spontaneous travel and disappearing up a mountain, rolled up in carpets, in the back of a lorry driven by a couple of terrorists: well... it's what we do.

Tim and I weren't without conflict zone experience. I'd already covered the Iran-Iraq war during the 1980s and others including Saddam's invasion of Kuwait in 1990.

'We dodged a bullet last time, so why not give the old wheel of fortune another spin?' is how Tim and I, perhaps foolishly, rationalised our decision.

Minutes later, both of us were bouncing around in the back of a truck, wrapped up in carpets like a couple of Swiss rolls, heading up a mountain track towards a secret PKK base.

After about thirty minutes the truck screeched to a stop and we heard a verbal altercation in Turkish between driver, Harjar, and other raised male voices.

From within my carpet cocoon I surmised we'd run into a

Turkish Army roadblock.

I was right.

As the argument intensified, Harjar stepped hard on the gas and the truck lurched off at breakneck speed. I thought I heard shots fired at us as we zigzagged away and up the mountain track.

From inside my carpet I yelled to young Tim: 'You OK, mate?'

'Never better, John,' came the stoic response from a cameraman who was generally one of life's unfazed.

For some reason the Turkish soldiers didn't make chase. Whether they couldn't be bothered, or Harjar and his comrade had convinced them they were local farmers, I don't know, but we'd soon put distance between us and the army checkpoint.

Twenty minutes later the truck braked and Harjar and his pal got out and hoisted Tim and I, still wrapped in carpets, onto the track where they rolled us out gasping for breath in the chill night air.

While we both enjoyed the rush of oxygen and release from our carpet wrapping, our escorts changed out of jeans and t-shirts and into the PKK's olive, military fatigues. The remainder of the journey to the PKK base was on foot, at times on hands and knees.

Four of us crawled up an unforgiving scree slope for about a half hour by torchlight, until we reached a makeshift PKK mountain base.

Their camp was among oak trees, which had grown bended over by the prevailing east wind. At ground level thorn bushes caught on our clothes. There were a dozen or so olive green tents used either as sleeping quarters or storage for thousands of rounds of ammunition packed in boxes with Russian markings.

Elsewhere the guerrillas had stretched tarpaulins between tree branches to give shelter for a kitchen, with a gas-fired stove and a general mess area. We'd arrived at one of the PKK's temporary forward operating bases from which they mounted lightning attacks on the Turkish Army in the valleys below - the same soldiers we'd encountered earlier.

Harjar and his pal kissed male comrades on both cheeks in the brotherly style of the region and, greetings over, I asked to speak to their commander.

'Welcome,' growled Marwan, a jowly, war weary, Kurdish fighter in his mid-forties, who'd wandered over.

I told him I was very keen to speak on camera to the two Western hostages: Rowbottom and Miller.

'Eat first,' responded Marwan, who gestured towards tureens of mutton and rice on wooden tables a few paces away. Some of his fighters already sat cross-legged under trees tucking into dinner.

I was desperate to get our interviews in the can and a news report filed from Ankara, before broadcast rivals BBC and ITN, who also had camera crews in the region, had a chance to catch up.

I pressed Marwan again.

'Sorry, Mr John... Mr David and Miss Tanya were here, but we moved them to another place,' he said without further elaboration.

Marwan was a man of few words and no amount of pleading – even me lying it was my birthday and I faced the sack from Sky News if I didn't get the interviews – was going to change his mind.

'Why don't you speak to my fighters and report about them instead?' he suggested.

Unique among insurgent groups in the Middle East, a third of the PKK fighters were female with waist length, raven hair platted into rainbow head bandanas - the ratio of PKK women fighting in Syria, southern Turkey and northern Iraq is around the same today.

They and their male companions were mostly in their twenties and thirties; overall a handsome bunch with sallow complexions, jet black hair and identically dressed in grey green military fatigues with AK47s strung across their shoulders.

I like to have an informal chat before an on-camera interview to break the ice, but they were a tough crowd, as they say in showbiz. I knew they were passionate followers of the communist Titan Karl Marx, however I didn't expect them to be utterly brainwashed and unable to converse about anything other than the late Mr K and his anti-capitalist musings.

As Tim's camera rolled, I asked Axin, a young guerrilla, what her family thought of her fighting a deadly, hot war against the might of the Turkish Army.

'Do your folks worry about you?' I inquired.

She shrugged her shoulders and launched into a rant about how her life was dedicated to: 'the overthrow of capitalism through a socialist revolution,' and how her earthly duty was: 'to smash the hated the class system. I don't care what my mother and father think, my duty is to follow the philosophies of Karl Marx,' she parroted.

Another female fighter, Ruken, delivered a tirade about the evils of capitalism and then revealed she was a sniper – she'd shot a Turkish soldier dead earlier in the day.

'I got him cleanly in the head. He just dropped down,' she said without emotion.

The male fighters were equally hooked on Marx. My attempt to lighten the mood with a chat about a recent Real Madrid-Barcelona football game fell on deaf ears. Marx meant more to them than Messi.

What was also odd: none of those glassy eyed, young guerrillas raised so much as a flicker of a smile or made any attempt to engage with Tim and I as we moved around the camp. It was if we were invisible to them.

I understood their rock solid commitment to the cause, but their aloofness was strange to me because Kurds in general tend to be sociable and inquisitive in the company of foreigners, especially a Western reporter and cameraman.

For sure, being constantly bombed by Turkish warplanes and witnessing companions being shot or blown to bits would have taken a severe mental toll, but as we wrapped up filming I couldn't fathom why they were so downcast.

Something wasn't quite right.

I concluded their general melancholy was because there was no clear end to their war against the Turks; no demob day to look forward to.

It wasn't until years later I watched a French television documentary, which uncovered evidence once PKK fighters had joined a unit - that was it. They were pretty much locked in for years. Leave was very limited and they risked being shot by their own comrades if they deserted.

The film also uncovered compelling testimony from those fighters who'd escaped and found sanctuary, that female PKK members were frequently subject to sexual abuse.

If the melancholy young men and women we met in the Taurus Mountains were effectively prisoners and perhaps being abused, as the French documentary suggested, it would have explained so much.

A PKK patrol

Female PKK fighters

2. Wounded guerrilla on board

By first light Tim and I had recorded some decent interviews, Tim had also shot some general views of camp life and a piece to camera from me.

Although I'd not been able film an interview with the two kidnapped travellers, Rowbottom and Miller, it was the first time a Western news crew had filmed with the PKK in one of their active bases, so I was happy with our exclusive.

As we were packing our gear, I heard what I thought was the rumble of thunder rolling around the mountains. Commander Marwan warned the ominous noise wasn't a storm but prowling Turkish warplanes; his fighters had to hide- ASAP.

As the guerrillas dismantled the camp and fled to nearby caves, Tim and I grabbed the camera gear, shouted our farewells and slithered down scree slope after scree slope, until, breathless and exhausted, we reached the village below, where that ill-starred Sky News assignment in east Turkey was about to take an unusual twist.

At the foot of the mountain we met up with taxi driver Mehmet, a jovial, plump Turk in his mid-fifties, who'd been waiting for us in a village by pre-arrangement.

We piled in the cab, Mehmet put his foot down and we were soon rattling towards the regional capital Diyarbakir, a hundred and fifty kilometres away where we'd already established a base at the Kervansaray Hotel. The idea was to stay that night, collect our gear and clothes and then fly on to Ankara the next day.

Mehmet's speed worried Tim and I, but we relaxed after a while knowing there's a fatalism attached to journeys in the Middle East which are always undertaken in an agreeable gamble with *Allah* called *enshallah,* or by the will of God.

Under the concept of *enshallah* it's preordained whether you'll arrive at your destination in one piece. If *Allah* wants you to arrive safely: you will.

Alternatively, if it's your fate to drive off a cliff, there's nothing you can do to avoid the inevitable, so if you're a driver you might as well put your foot down.

And talking of happenstance: as we bowled along eastern Turkey's undulating countryside a hundred or so paces ahead a young female in military fatigues suddenly staggered out from bushes and collapsed on the verge.

Mehmet braked and the three of us leapt out of the taxi.

She was in her early twenties and a PKK fighter. She had a stomach wound and by the look of a growing blood stain on the front of her tunic she clearly needed urgent medical attention. We eased her into the front seat of Mehmet's taxi and her lips resembled a half smile as she mumbled incoherently in Kurdish.

But what to do with a shot Kurdish fighter in Turkish controlled territory?

We stopped at a Kurdish farmhouse where I was able to telephone my PKK contact in the oddly named city of Batman to say we were on our way with an injured fighter in need of a doctor.

After more than thirty years in the business I've developed a supreme faith in a deity who keeps a benevolent eye on journalists going about their lawful business in risky situations. He/

she must have intervened because we encountered no Turkish Army roadblocks and we handed the injured young woman over to her comrades, close to the spot outside Batman where we'd met our PKK escorts the day before.

Months later, I heard from the PKK that the young woman had been wounded in a mountain shoot-out with Turkish soldiers and she'd staggered down to the valleys, where we'd picked her up.

I also learned after doctors patched her up she'd re-joined her guerrilla unit, to continue the fight. Whether she'd had any choice in returning to the fray is not known.

But if we'd thought the long arm of the Turkish security services had done with us, we were wrong. We arrived at the Kervansaray Hotel in Diyarbakir, in the early hours.

The hotel is known locally, in English, as 'The Inn of Evil,' perhaps because it looks like a grey stone, medieval prison from the outside - although it's provided welcome accommodation since 1521 for Silk Road traders and pilgrims making the long trek to Mecca. Beyond the giant, wooden front door was a courtyard and stabling for eight-hundred camels. We said our goodbyes to driver Mehmet and approached the middle-aged night porter sitting at reception who barely looked up from his newspaper as he handed Tim and I our bedroom keys in a desultory fashion.

We then trudged wearily upstairs to our stone-clad, window-less bedrooms hoping for a good sleep only to be faced with a shocking scene.

Drawers had been turned out; clothes and broadcast equipment had been tossed everywhere. Our beds had been stripped. Feathers spewed out of torn pillows. My notes and a couple of books were torn and scattered to the four winds.

I went down to reception to confront the clerk.

'You been working with the PKK, my friend.' muttered the clerk, his eyes still fixed on the sports pages. 'The police... they been looking for you.'

Tim and I flew on to Ankara the next day with no further aggravation from the Turkish security services.

Maybe they'd tapped my phone calls to London that night and lost interest in us when they'd heard me tell my editor we'd failed to locate and interview kidnap victims, Rowbottom and Miller, both of whom were released by the PKK in mid-August 1993 – around four weeks after our fruitless search.

At a press conference in the Turkish capital the pair denied succumbing to Stockholm Syndrome, but admitted they'd struck up a sympathetic relationship with their PKK captors.

They said they understood what their kidnappers were fighting for and how they'd had empathy with them - words which wouldn't have sat well with the Turkish government.

Ms Miller told reporters she and her companion had: 'marched with PKK fighters through mountains, night after night,' and she described how they'd survived rocket attacks by Turkish warplanes.

She said she had a gash below her knee from stumbling against a tree during one night march, and both she and her companion had been very sick.

Perhaps they'd been ill when Tim and I went searching for them and that's why Marwan prevented us meeting them.

'It's all sinking in,' Ms Miller told the press conference.

Still traumatised, she gripped Mr Rowbottom's hand and added, 'We've had to do a lot of holding hands to make it through.'

3. Welcome back Mr John.

Low cloud often rolls in from the wild grille of the Zagros mountains and Erbil airport was under a grey shroud as my Austrian Airlines plane began its final approach.

I eased back in my window seat and waited for the familiar thump of wheels on the runway, meanwhile my mind drifted back to countless previous assignments to Iraq, a country which has featured hugely in my journalistic life through decades of conflict and the occasional peaceful years when they put their guns away.

Flying in and out of Iraq has always been a piquant and agreeably exciting experience because you never quite know how the trip is going to pan out - it's that kind of country.

But first, you've got to get on the ground safely.

In the years immediately after the 2003 US-led invasion of Iraq Sunni jihadis routinely fired heat-seeking missiles at foreign commercial and military planes, so pilots were forced to use a highly unconventional, 'corkscrew' landing method for airports like Erbil, Baghdad and Basrah.

Say you were flying in to Erbil: the captain would do a couple of very tight, tilting laps of the airport at 10,000 feet and after circling for a while and getting the all clear to land he'd suddenly flip the flaps sending the plane into a Space Mountain nosedive.

You felt the G-force kick in and your ears popped; seats and the fuselage creaked alarmingly; passengers' white knuckles clutched vibrating arms rests.

But a few loop-the-loops later the runway suddenly appeared and... ccrrunch! You'd landed.

And more often than not, just as your plane spiralled down, another aircraft had taken off below and was 'corkscrewing' skywards. At mid-point – somewhere between heaven and earth – two giant silver birds danced an aerial *pas de deux* and you held your breath.

Commercial pilots who were more used spending hours on autopilot across oceans, loved the thrill of 'corkscrew' landings and called it 'real flying,' although it was squeaky bottom time for recently recruited Iraqi air traffic controllers – if they could even bear to watch their radar screens.

And perils associated with flying in and out of Iraq didn't end once you were on the ground.

Airport buildings were, and still are, a target for bomb, rocket and gun attack. In 2020/21, Erbil came under rocket fire and Baghdad was fired on multiple times by Shia militias aiming at the US military base next to the main terminal.

Several times I've sat holding my boarding pass in various Iraqi departure lounges, looking forward to flying home, when mortar explosions have rattled chandeliers and sent souvenir vendors and passengers running for cover – me included.

On one occasion I was aboard an Iraqi Airways 737 out of Erbil in 2003 which was so packed with refugee families it was standing room only at the back.

And as the overloaded Boeing strained every rivet to crawl into the skies there was horrible, metallic noise as its belly scraped the lights at the end of the runway.

I'm happy to say we landed safely at our destination of Amman.

Another memory: I was on an Emirates flight, parked at the gate in Baghdad in 2012 waiting to push back, when an unknown terror group gained air-side access and sprayed the jet's tail fin with machine gun bullets.

Remarkably, not a single passenger was injured and even more astonishing: there was no panic on board.

Just another day in the life of Baghdad International.

We landed at Erbil more or less on time, despite poor visibility. When I first started travelling to the Kurdistan region, more than thirty years ago, the old airport used to be no more than a humpback of a runway and a huddle of Nissen huts.

But the new airport, which opened in 2005, is impressive; designed by the British firm Scott Wilson and constructed at a cost of half a billion US dollars by the Turkish company Makyol Cengiz. First time visitors are surprised because it looks much the same as any airport in the West – but there's nothing normal about Erbil. Its runway is 270 feet wide and three miles in length making it one of the world's longest and able to accommodate the American Air Force's biggest planes: the giant Boeing B-52 bombers.

Erbil has to shut down from time to time when conflict flares in the region. In 2015, when Russian warships in the Caspian Sea fired missiles through Kurdish airspace to hit targets in Syria, the Reuters news agency reported this glorious understatement from the frustrated Kurdish Government:

'The cabinet of the Kurdistan Region of Iraq called on the Russian government to find alternative routes as soon as possible for its rockets passing over Kurdish airspace, including over Erbil.'

And a reminder Erbil airport is in a tough neighbourhood: as my Austrian Airlines flight trundled towards the main passenger terminal I spotted half a dozen Chinook helicopters parked on one of the aprons. They'd been in action the day before ferrying US special forces on their mission to assassinate Islamic State leader Abu Bakir al-Baghdadi. The assault had ended with the jihadi chief blowing himself up – former President Donald Trump had declared Al Baghdadi had 'died like a dog'.

As our plane neared the Chinooks a flight attendant hit the Tannoy button and cautioned, 'ladies and gentlemen: photography is forbidden at this airport.'

She was too late. I and other passengers had already snapped an image on our iPhones.

At the luggage carousel I studied the faces of travellers who'd been on my flight. They were mostly Iraqi and Syrian Kurds returning home from visiting relatives in Europe.

They clutched cheap suitcases with one arm and the other arm was wrapped around DVD players, Play Stations, laptops and other 'tech' gadgets they'd bought in London, Paris, Frankfurt and Vienna.

Tired and fractious kids dawdled behind mums and dads.

There was also a sprinkling of East European security contractors and half a dozen young Western aid workers bound for Kurdistan's burgeoning refugee camps.

There were only ten flights in that day, but fifteen years earlier Erbil's arrivals hall was very different.

Plane after plane disgorged a seething mass who'd flown from all over the world to grab a slice of what they thought would be Klondike Kurdistan. Suited up entrepreneurs with slicked hair, Gucci briefcases and millions in venture capital to burn, rubbed shoulders with roided up security men from Dallas, Doncaster and Dortmund, all hoping to make a fast buck before hightailing it out of Dodge.

How naive they'd been.

Few of them knew how to prise open the dead hand of Kurdish bureaucracy, or which ministry man to bribe; most got burned and returned home thousands of dollars poorer having learned a painful lesson: Kurdistan - and Iraq in general - is a very tough gig. Even major Western corporations with a long track record in Iraq, like US oil Titans Exxon Mobil and Chevron, have scaled back over the years. Sky-high insurance and demands from corrupt Kurdish politicians wanting eye watering pay-offs became too much.

But Russian, Turk, Lebanese and Emirati company bosses: they understood how to untangle Kurdish red tape. They knew whose palm to grease. They won the big contracts in Kurdistan – and still do. And it will be the same savvy corporations from those countries who will explore Kurdistan's undeveloped gas fields and excavate the region's vast, untapped mineral wealth including gold and platinum - once the decades old minefields have been cleared.

What about the Chinese, you might be thinking? Surely they've been sniffing around? The Chinese only invest when it's to their advantage and they've yet to arrive in Iraqi Kurdistan a major way - although Beijing recently appointed a consul general who was warmly welcomed by President Nechirvan Barzani, whilst I was there in late 2019, so it won't be long before Beijing's tentacles tighten their grip around Kurdistan's unexplored wealth.

As the late afternoon sun melted into the horizon and the

air chilled, I joined the modest queue outside arrivals for a taxi into town where I chatted to a lone Austrian businessman who'd been on my flight. We got talking about lack of Western investment in Kurdistan.

'You know how things work here. It's all about bribing the right people' said Lucas.

'But these days Western company directors are scared, because it's much more likely they'll be prosecuted in their home countries for corruption and handed big jail terms under UK or US laws. It's not like the old days, when law enforcement turned a blind eye. For me putting any serious money into Kurdistan, is more like adventure capital, not venture capital,' he went on, hoping I'd appreciate his little joke.

Lucas was right of course. Bribery and corruption is as insidious and as rampant as ever in Iraq and Western corporations are investing elsewhere.

I wished Lucas well and dived into my cab where I flicked on my cellphone.

Telecoms provider Asiacell flashed, 'Welcome to the cradle of civilisation.'

It was good to be back!

4. Downtown

I wasn't travelling on a news channel's expense account; I'd paid for the trip myself, so with some regret I told my cab driver to forget the luxury Diwan hotel, the Rotana or the Hyatt Regency off the airport road.

Instead I picked out the modest Altin Saray Hotel, a Turkish owned establishment in Iskan Street in downtown Erbil - a bargain I thought, at thirty dollars a night.

Within half an hour we'd pulled up outside and I hopped in.

Receptionist Dani, a Syrian Kurd who'd recently fled his war-ravaged homeland, photocopied my passport and faxed it - yes, they still have fax machines - to the Kurdish Government's security services.

Job done, he started fumbling for a bedroom key beneath the counter.

'Mr John: cancel your booking through the internet company. Thirty dollars a night is far too expensive. You can have a room here at my beautiful hotel for twenty five US, if you pay me cash. I'll throw in breakfast.'

'Deal,' I said.

'And, Mr John, I'll give you room 512...'

'...It's one of our cleanest,' he whispered confidentially.

'Welcome back to Kurdistan.'

The lift up to the bedrooms was a monster.

Once you stepped inside and pressed the button to ascend its metal doors started to slide shut at tortoise speed, but at the last minute they jammed and left a gap of about an inch, meaning the lift couldn't budge.

Guests were expected to squeeze the doors together using both hands until they suddenly snapped shut with an alarming crack, like a crocodile's jaws. I nearly lost my fingers the first time!

My bedroom was low-end Levant, circa 1970: psychedelic, floral curtains which weren't broad enough to meet in the middle no matter how hard you tugged; an air-con system that blew hot, not cold; a 'fridge door that wouldn't shut because a mini iceberg had grown around the freezer cabinet and I got a mild electric shock from the shower control knob. Apart from that, the room was fine.

After I'd unpacked I plodded about half a mile to the city's heart: the magnificent Citadel which, at seven thousand years old, is twice the age of the Great Pyramids at Giza.

The castle walls have largely been rebuilt, so they're not strictly authentic, but when the mass tourism comes to Kurdistan - one day in the far future - visiting Westerners will surely marvel at the towering brown-brick ramparts which dominate the city's old quarter and are magnificent.

I wandered down to the main square, past cafes where men in traditional salwar pants and turbans gossiped and sipped tea beneath paintings of Kurdish *peshmerga* fighters from another age.

Off the main square I ambled along my favourite part of the old city at night: ancient alleyways thick with billowing clouds of blue-grey smoke from sizzling kebab stalls; a timeless warren of hissing gas lamps and excitement where adults and their kids stood in wide-eyed wonder before great vats of ice creams in pastel shades and where housewives bartered over boxes of plump dates, nuts and exotic spices. The smells and sights in that ancient maze always overwhelms the senses.

A few paces away I found another noisy puzzle of alleys where errand boys whistled and yelled out as they pushed rickety carts for their masters piled with boxes of fruit and vegetables.

They dodged with great skill between groups of families out shopping and between wooden trestle tables groaning under every consumable you could imagine: mountains of jeans, socks, pants and knickers, piles of toiletries such as shampoos, toothpaste, hair-dye and lipsticks and costume jewellery, fake Rolexes and pirated DVDs.

I walked on past vendors selling glittering, live goldfish.

And had I been looking for something as unlikely as an electric pump? - no problem. Shops in one alley, sold nothing else.

Another stocked only paraffin heaters.

Yet another was a plumber's paradise of baths, sinks and taps in silver, gold and bronze.

The Citadel and souks were surely as noisy, atmospheric and as amaranthine as I'd always known them, but I noticed one difference from my visit two years before.

The crumbling two storey Ottoman houses that had nuzzled around the feet of the Citadel for centuries - symbolic of Erbil's multicultural past - had been bulldozed and cleared. The new was swallowing the old.

And in the far distance: a sprawl of new hotels, malls and freeways alongside which freshly-built apartment blocks had sprouted like topsy bearing names synonymous with Edwardian Britain like: Empire Royal Apartments, the English Village

Compound and Park View.

I didn't need to ask the locals what they thought about the loss of their cultural heritage. I'm sure most welcomed the new builds because, broadly speaking, Middle Easterners tend to live in the here and now. For them new is good and I know few tears, if any, would have been shed about losing remnants of the past.

As I wandered back to my hotel I reminded myself of the time I first began reporting from the region when the Kurds lived under the jackboot of Saddam's genocidal rule.

Back then I could never have imagined the poor, persecuted Kurds would one day be dining in Pizza Hut or a KFC, or shopping in a Carrefour, enjoying multiplex cinemas or having anywhere near enough cash to rent or buy an apartment in a towering complex called the Empire Royal.

Emotionally, it was quite overwhelming for me and my heart sang for the Kurdish people.

For some reason I always sleep well in Iraq, even in the dark years after the US led invasion in 2003 when car bombs outside hotels blew guests like me out of bed, usually around first light.

That night at the Altin Saray Hotel I turned in early, wrapped a single blanket over me, stared at the stars through the curtains that wouldn't close... and slept like a baby.

5. Who are the Kurds?

I'd arrived in Erbil just a few weeks after Donald Trump announced he was withdrawing American military support for Kurdish fighters who'd played a key role in Syria defeating the jihadists of Islamic State.

Trump had also effectively given a green light to Turkey's President Erdogan to invade northern Syria, home to hundreds of thousands of Kurds. The former American president's decisions had outraged the Kurds, not only because Kurdish communities in north Syria were left in great peril, they were also furious Trump had added to their misery by making disparaging remarks about the Kurds on the world stage.

During an Oval Office meeting with the Italian President, Trump turned to the cameras and described the Kurds as 'no angels'.

Trump then added, 'They (Kurds) fought with us. We paid a lot of money for them to fight with us and that's OK. They did well when they fought with us. They didn't do so well when they didn't fight with us. They've got a lot of sand over there. So, there's a lot of sand that they can play with. Let them fight their own wars.'

Trump's surprise abandonment of the Kurds had sent newspaper and television editors scrambling to commission articles and video reports along the lines of: 'Who are the Kurds?'

Sitting in a tea shop in Iskan Street, on my first full day in Erbil, I also Googled: 'Who are the Kurds?' just out of curiosity.

My laptop screen filled with dozens of entries from a plethora of news outlets including the Washington Post, The Times and Channel 9 Australia et al. It was mostly cut and paste pap, rushed out at the last minute - nothing in depth.

'Who are the Kurds? What kind of headline is that?' grumbled Shivan Fazil, a good friend whom I'd joined for a glass of mint tea.

'It's so freaking patronising,' he moaned.

'It's like asking: who are the Scots, or who are the Irish? Why doesn't the world already know the Kurds were key players in the history of human civilisation? Don't those fools in the Western media know the Kurds have been around for at least nine millennia... the beginning of time, when the wheel, algebra and writing were being invented. "Who are the Kurds?" What a question, what a cheek!

They can piss right off!'

I understood his anger.

But, Shivan, my friend, I can tell you researching the origins of the Kurdish people is hard going, because there are no reliable records going back far enough. The only fact historians can point to is the Kurds are thought to be of Indo-European descent, nomadic by nature, ethnically close to present-day Iranians. And they are definitely not Arab.

The most famous Kurd in history was Saladin, a Muslim general who successfully beat the European crusader armies in the twelfth century AD.

But going back further than Saladin takes researchers into very murky waters because chroniclers of ancient history, like Herodotus, Livy and Tacitus weren't around nine thousand years ago, when it's believed the Kurds emerged as a distinct ethnic group. With a lack of reliable sources, you're left with nothing much more than myths and legends.

For example: there was the fabulously wealthy and wise King Solomon - he of the Hebrew Bible - who lived around 900 BC and was also known in non-biblical circles as a magician and exorcist.

Legend has it the King controlled a pack of unruly genies whom he dispatched to Europe to find 500 beautiful women to grace the regal harem. The genies got distracted and took so long in their quest, by the time they got back the King was dead!

So, the spirits married the women themselves, settled in the Zagros Mountains and called themselves Kurds.

That's one story. Then, there's this: there was an evil Assyrian king called Zahak, who had two snakes growing out of his shoulders.

One of weirdo Zahak's demands was a young man be killed every day and his brains be cooked and served to him for lunch. The chefs took pity on one youth, saved his life and served the King a sheep's brain instead. The King didn't notice the difference.

Meanwhile, the lad fled to the mountains where he formed an army and killed mad King Zahak. Afterwards he created a community, known as the Kurds.

And there's more. In the seventeenth century an Armenian chronicler called Mighdisi wrote about a King Kurdim, a member of the same community as the prophet Noah.

According to Mighdisi: King Kurdim reigned for an incredible 600 years and settled in the Kurdistan region, where he: 'begat many children and descendants,' called Kurds.

However, there is one story about the origins of the Kurds which has a ring of truth. In fact it's regarded as so authentic, the Kurdish Regional Government has used a line from it for the Kurdish national anthem. The first line of the fourth verse reads: *We are the descendants of the Medes and Cyaxares.*

Bingo! There it is, in black and white.

So, who were the Medes and who was Cyaxares?

The Median Kingdom flourished in the eighth century BC, during the time of the Iron Age in Europe. It was centred in central and western Iran, but spread to include what was then all Persia, most of modern-day Turkey, Armenia and Turkmenistan.

The Medians' religion was Zoroastrian, one of humanity's oldest faiths: good thoughts, good words, good deeds.

Cyaxares (pronounced Kay-kus-row) was hailed by the ancients and successive scholars since, as the greatest of all the Median kings. His prowess as a military man is well documented by Greek chronicler Herodotus in his tome: 'The Histories,' from which we learned Cyaxares split his army into ranks of spearmen, archers and horsemen. No ancient leader had done that before. They went on to conquer all before them, making the Median Kingdom a regional power.

The Kurdish militia, the *peshmerga,* enjoy a reputation as formidable fighters, as do various Kurdish separatist guerrilla groups. So maybe the bellicose Kurds really did inherit the genes of an ancient king and their true origins do lie in the Median dynasty.

I'd like to think so.

6. Hoshayar

I'm not sure how long I've known Hoshayar Zebari, possibly thirty years; I've lost count. Although not a household name in the US or Europe, Hoshayar is a well-known and respected politician in the Middle East having been Iraq's Foreign Minister for more than ten years.

He's a thoughtful man who enjoys gossiping with foreign journalists and, crucially, he's one of those rare politicians who understands we scribblers/broadcasters have a difficult job making sense of the region's complexity, where nothing is quite what it seems.

In a society where family ties are important, I should point out: Hoshayar is uncle to a former Kurdish Regional Government President, and great uncle to the current one. Being so well connected, he's a terrific Middle East contact.

He was kind enough to invite me to his home during a visit in late 2019 and he was on fine form when we met at his villa in Saluhdin; an eagle's nest of residences for Kurdistan's political and business elite midway up a mountain, about thirty minutes in a fast cab from Erbil.

His eyes sparkled as he proudly showed me he'd lost a dramatic amount of weight following a medical procedure and strict diet.

'I had to do something John, I was a bit obese, as you know,' he grinned. 'Now look at me!'

I had to agree. He was literally half his former self, at least in girth.

Like many old school Kurdish politicians Hoshayar was *peshmerga* fighter in his youth - historically a guerrilla force which spearheaded revolts against successive Iraqi governments, especially Saddam Hussein's. After Saddam was deposed he became Iraq's Foreign Minister from 2003 until 2014, then Deputy Prime Minister, before being appointed Finance Minister.

Over coffee and sweet cakes - so much for his diet - and with the flames of a gas fire dancing in his living room hearth, he explained he'd just returned from Baghdad to advise Iraqi President Barham Saleh how to handle protests over corruption and mismanagement of the economy.

When he and I spoke the independent High Commission for Human Rights in Iraq had reported 319 protestors had been shot dead by Iraqi security forces and 15,000 injured - by mid-2020 fatalities had risen to around 500.

'Iraq has been smouldering for years,' said Hoshayar sadly. 'Now, it's as if someone has thrown gasoline on it.'

I asked him who was behind the unrest: was it Iran?

'Some are blaming Iran for stoking tensions to weaken the government. I don't believe that,' he said.

'Why would Iran try to collapse a regime it has built up? It doesn't make sense. No, outside forces are not involved,' added Hoshayar. 'Unrest is home grown. Iraqi youths in cities like Baghdad, Najaf and Basrah are on the streets because they see corruption all around, and no future.

Protestors know the danger but seem to have no fear of being shot dead. They're dying because they think they have nothing to lose. It's very sad.'

I asked him why Iraq's traditional allies like America and

Britain hadn't intervened, other than issuing general statements condemning the violence.

'Oh, forget the British,' sighed Hoshayar. 'No one takes Britain seriously these days. They used to be big players in the Middle East, but London's influence is negligible now.'

'The Americans are different,' he continued. 'They still wield great influence and I've been urging the US Ambassador in Baghdad to speak out more strongly against the harsh crackdown on protesters.

As you say, the US Embassy issues statements calling for restraint from time to time, but it's not enough. They need to go further and put real pressure on the government.'

Our conversation switched to the summer of 2014 when Iraqi Kurdistan almost fell under the control of one of the world's most brutal terror groups: Islamic State.

Bankrolled by phenomenally wealthy Saudi Arabian and Qatari oil sheikhs, Islamic State had become one of the richest and best-armed terror groups on the planet.

Commercially important cities like Raqqa in Syria and Al-Faluja and Al-Ramadi in Iraq had fallen to the jihadists, along with the Kurds' spiritual home: oil-rich Kirkuk.

Islamic State's huge success was partly because they were highly motivated and well-armed in what they saw as a holy war, but also because of their uniquely successful attack strategy.

Once they had a village, town or city in their sights they opened an assault with waves of suicide bombers to kill and demoralise the local military defenders. Then, they hit their targets with tanks and rockets.

Having seized a village or town, the jihadists terrified locals by executing police, administrative officials and random men off the street, usually by beheading, although some they hanged or set on fire.

And when the initial horror show was over, they locked the town they'd just overwhelmed under the iron grip of Sharia Law - then they'd push on to seize another community.

In August 2014 Islamic State had risen to the height of their powers having captured territory in Iraq and Syria the size of Finland; home to eight million people. Oil fields and refineries, vast grain stores and some of the region's most lucrative smuggling routes had all fallen under their control.

Their leader, Abu Baker Al-Baghdadi, famously delivered his victory speech and climbed the steps of the thousand-year old Al Nouri Mosque in Mosul and did something Osama Bin Laden always promised to do, but failed: he declared a caliphate.

By August 8th 2014, Al-Baghdadi and his fanatical supporters, had set their sights on the glittering prize of Iraqi Kurdistan's de facto capital, Erbil.

In the days before Kurdish *peshmerga* fighters had fought to defend a front-line of about a hundred and fifty miles, but against well-equipped, battle-hardened Islamic State fighters the woefully under-equipped Kurdish militiamen had no choice but to make a tactical retreat to defend Erbil.

Islamic State paused their advance just 20 miles from the city to regroup and aim their big guns.

There was a catch of emotion in Hoshayar's voice as he recounted the night of August 8th 2014 when he was summoned from his home to a Kurdish military command centre in Saluhdin, to join members of the KDP leadership.

'I will never forget that terrible evening,' said Hoshayar.

'I stepped outside the command centre and looked towards Erbil. There were streams of car headlights leaving the city, as far as my eye could see. It was like a scene from a disaster movie as people tried to escape the coming Islamic State onslaught,' he recalled. 'And yes: I was frightened.'

Kurdish leaders had already received intelligence an attack on Erbil was imminent.

'I panicked. I knew we couldn't defend the city on our own' said Hoshayar. 'We needed outside help; more specifically American assistance; very quickly.'

But was Washington going to help, that was the big question? The US had scaled back support for the Iraqi Kurds after they announced plans for an independence referendum. A breakaway Kurdistan was an anathema to the Obama administration which believed in a united federal Iraq.

Despite a chill in relations between Washington and Erbil, Hoshayar decided to use his good contacts with US military chiefs and politicians to beg for help to save Kurdistan.

'I called US Secretary of State John Kerry, first,' he said.

'I told him Erbil was about to fall and tried to make him understand how urgently we needed American military help. Kerry listened carefully, but was non-committal.

I also telephoned Vice-President Joe Biden and the chairman of the joint chiefs, General Dempsey.'

Hoshayar added: 'I remember I actually yelled down the phone to Dempsey. I begged him to come to Kurdistan's rescue, saying: it's not a matter of days, it's hours before Erbil is taken. I shouted down the line we needed American military help.'

Dempsey decided to act, but he explained any US military strikes would need approval from Obama himself and the President was with his wife at a dinner engagement in Washington.

'Dempsey must have understood how desperate the situation was and he managed to get a message to Obama, who then hurried back to the White House and the Situation Room,' said Hoshayar.

'Thank God, Obama authorised a US military air-strike on Islamic State's two main gun positions outside Erbil.'

Obama's strike orders were the first significant US battlefield role in Iraq since the last American combat soldier left the country at the end of 2011. So, America's intervention that night was a major shift in policy for the Obama Administration.

At the time Obama justified his action to critics in Congress by saying the imminent threat to Erbil and the unfolding dire humanitarian situation in nearby Sinjar province met his criteria for deploying American forces.

He also argued he was protecting US lives, presumably including those in the American Consulate in Erbil.

Within hours of Hoshayar's SOS to Washington, US Navy F-18 fighters and Predator drones dropped 500-pound laser-guided bombs on a number of Islamic State targets, including one on a mobile artillery piece which had already begun shelling Erbil.

Pentagon spokesman, Rear Admiral John Kirby, told reporters Islamic State fighters had been 'successfully eliminated'.

Hoshayar paused for a moment of reflection and said: 'We came very close to disaster that night, however, when I heard the American air strikes were underway I knew I could go to bed and have a good sleep!

Did my frantic phone calls to Washington help save

Kurdistan from being overrun by Islamic State? Well I guess I did play a small part saving us... yes,' said my old Kurdish friend, with a smile.

7. Iskan Street

It was getting late and Hoshayar had asked his driver to run me back to my hotel in downtown Erbil.

As the limousine glided silently down a switchback of roads from the mountain tops of Saluhdin, the wide plains below glowed a soft white beneath a mosaic of crystal stars and the Moon's watery sphere.

On the far horizon the lights of Erbil shimmered like strings of diamonds.

It was one of those delicious moments known only to travellers to Iraq; a split second in time when you're suddenly struck by the majesty of that ancient land, its unparalleled place in humanity's history and its profound beauty.

But, let's not be too dewy-eyed over Mesopotamia.

Across the centuries, countless foreign invaders have brought death, chaos and misrule to the people who live there.

The Persians, the Romans, Hulagu Khan and his Mongol hordes, Ottoman and British imperialists, American-led Western armies, Al-Qaeda jihadists and the brutal fascists of Islamic State have all invaded; few on Earth have suffered under the sword as much as the Mesopotamians; the very earth beneath their feet is soaked in the blood of their ancestors.

And yet, despite the horrors of history, or perhaps because of them, the people of this remarkable region are irrepressible spirits. Somehow, no matter how many times they get bombed, their homes and cities flattened and lives destroyed, they always struggle to their feet again and rebuild their shattered lives.

Hoshayar's driver dropped me close to my hotel in Iskan Street, where high-spirited Iraqi energy and sheer zest for life was in abundance.

It was ten o'clock at night, and a gang of Arab labourers, fresh in from Baghdad, had apparently been hired to demolish a derelict shop.

As they knocked seven bells out of the former grocery store with sledgehammers, clouds of white dust stuck to their ragged shirts, trousers and to their hair and grimacing faces - they looked like men who'd accidentally fallen into bags of flour.

And more street theatre close by: a wiry fellow in his twenties was performing a bit of spot-welding repair on a motorbike in the middle of the pavement, closely observed by a circle of curious bystanders crouched on their haunches.

But, Iskan Street's main attraction wasn't late night demolition or motorbike repairs.

It was the half mile or so of tea houses and fast food outlets which were packed with an all-male clientele. Each premises I dived into felt like a rugby club stag do, without the alcohol.

It's always been very difficult for me, as a Western man, to get my head around Middle Eastern social norms which require wives and children be left at home whilst menfolk enjoyed a night out, with other men. It doesn't feel right.

I chatted to Sirwan, a twenty-five year old, random tea house customer about what to me was the absurdity of the tacit ban on women and children.

'We like it.' he said.

'No women and kids around means we're free to talk about politics and football. We men can swear and be ourselves.'

I bade him a pleasant evening and resumed my stroll.

As I ambled along Iskan Street I noticed the tea house frontages had poetic names in Kurdish, such as 'The House of Summer' or 'My Father's Home'.

Each had gardens, illuminated with fairy lights where customers had crowded games tables.

Players in a high state of concentration sucked on hubble-bubble pipes and blew out clouds of fragrant, pastel grey smoke into the night air.

All were silent and focussed on the business in hand. The only sound was the sharp crack of dominoes being slammed down or the chunky roll of backgammon dice.

There was also another game being played. It originated in Turkey, it's called *Okey* and seemed the most popular.

To play a dealer dished out 106 little plastic tiles to four players or more. They kept their tiles on racks in front of them so opponents couldn't see what they'd got.

Long story short: the winner was the one with the least value tiles at the end of the game.

It was time to find something to eat and it was hard to miss one cafe with a huge vat on the pavement outside heated by a roaring gas burner.

Inside the bubbling cauldron was a whole skinned sheep, including skull and horns, half submerged in a bubbling yellowish broth.

I'm not a massive fan of boiled sheeps' brains/eyes/testicles, but the rest of the menu posted at the doorway looked delicious so I stepped inside and found myself a table.

I'd entered a Bedlam of shouting, sweating, hairy armed waiters who served up vast portions of skewered lamb and chicken smothered in tomatoes, onion and chillies, along with piles of *naan* bread on plastic trays.

To add to the general mayhem a TV blared above customers' heads, so everyone had to yell at each other to make themselves heard.

My selection of lamb kebabs had been an excellent choice, although if you can't find a decent kebab in a country like Iraq, you might as well give up!

Apart from tea houses and fast food outlets there were barbers where young blades waited patiently in line for the latest, fashionable cockscomb haircut, and electronics goods stores selling the newest in computers and mobile phones from the Far East.

Iskan Street's other big draw were sports cafes screening European football games on giant television sets.

It soon became clear: the bigger the screen and the louder the commentary volume the more customers the cafe attracted.

Like most Iraqis, Kurds are mad about football and because of the regional broadcasting rights the average footie-fan tends to support either of Spain's two top clubs: Barcelona or Real Madrid.

When the two teams played each other every season in a clash known as *El Classico*, passions boiled over and fist fights broke out in Iskan Street as rival fans slugged it out, or so one proprietor told me.

As I continued my walk Iskan Street seemed busy to me, but apparently it wasn't running at full tilt.

I found out why at a cafe called My Grandfather's House, when I chatted to a chubby cheeked, twenty-five-year-old waiter called Muzar, who was serving up sticky sweetmeats made of flour, sugar and milk on a vast silver tray.

He told me since 2014, when Islamic State fighters came with within twenty miles of the gates of Erbil, trade had slumped by a third and hadn't really recovered.

At the time of our conversation the jihadists had been pushed back by US and *peshmerga* military action to Makhmour, but that was only forty miles away.

'People are afraid,' said Muzar.

'The Arab guys still come here, but the Kurdish customers – and they are most of my trade – are hanging on to their money and staying at home,' he added with a frown.

'Despite what the politicians tell us Islamic State hasn't been defeated and they haven't gone away. The people know this.'

I wished him well and started to head back to my hotel, but not without stopping for another local ritual: a shoeshine.

At least a dozen shoeshine boys operated along Iskan Street, that's one lad to every hundred paces of pavement.

They perched on bar stools with the tools of their trade crammed into a biscuit tin; polishes ranging from jet black to light brown, dusters and brass handled brushes - stiff bristled to baby soft.

A smiley, curly haired ten year old in a ragged, blue checked shirt and scruffy jeans, who had two front teeth missing, beckoned me over and gestured me to remove my shoes.

I duly handed them over and, rather formally, he gave me a pair of bright yellow, plastic sandals in return and indicated I should sit down at a nearby cafe table, order a cup of chai and to return in ten minutes.

I did so and watched the lad's performance from a few paces away at one of the cafe's outside tables.

First, he waved his arms as theatrically as a concert *maestro* would as he daubed each shoe with unctuous black polish.

Then came the first of a series of buffings.

Yet more polishing followed, then an application of clear wax, and lashings of elbow grease.

When he paused it seemed an appropriate moment to step forward to retrieve my shiny shoes.

But no; it was only the interval.

With a mock frown the lad motioned me to return to my seat in the cafe and then, with much respect, he lowered my freshly polished shoes to the pavement.

Apparently they had to 'rest,' like a side of roast meat fresh from the oven.

After two minutes of 'resting' they got a final, grand buffing until they glistened like pair of Fred Astaire's patent leather, tap shoes.

I'd just watched a masterclass in the art of shoe polishing and for the whole performance he charged me the equivalent of one US dollar - it seemed right to tip him five.

It was after midnight, credits had already rolled on the big screen TVs and cafes and businesses turned off their lights; Iskan Street's customers began to look for their cars and head home to their wives and families.

The shoeshine lad snapped the lid shut on his biscuit tin and wished me a happy stay in Kurdistan.

Time for bed.

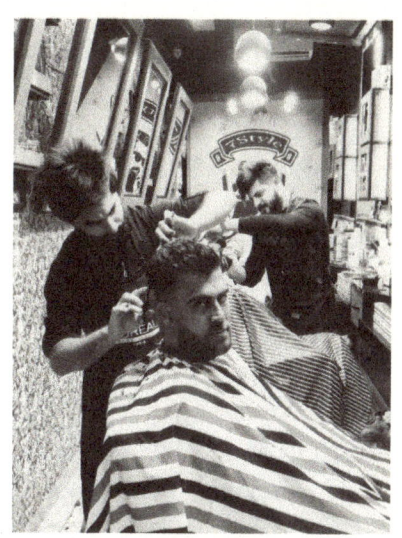

Barber shop, Iskan Street, Erbil

Kurdish men playing Okey, Iskan Street, Erbil

8. Christians in peril

Everyone who wants to live a godly life
in Christ Jesus will be persecuted.

TIMOTHY 3:12.

There was an armed guard on the front and rear gates at St Joseph's Church in the Ankawa district of Erbil.

'Mostly for show,' assured the Archbishop's aide with a smile as I stepped in.

Security was tight for a reason.

Six years before the jihadists of Islamic State had much of western Iraq including the Kurdish region, in their grip. More than 125,000 Christians, mainly Chaldean, had been brutally displaced from their homelands.

Countless thousands had been killed without mercy when they'd refused to renounce their faith.

Many families were left without shelter and refuge, work or their homes. Churches and monasteries had been blown up, leaving them with nothing that gave Christian life dignity: family visits, celebration of weddings and births, the sharing of sorrows.

'Although we're scourged and wounded, somehow we're still here,' said Archbishop Bashar Wardar a no nonsense, articulate Chaldean Church leader.

'In Iraq there's no redress for those who've lost properties, homes and businesses. Tens of thousands of Christians have nothing to show for their life's work, in places where their families have lived, maybe, for thousands of years.'

He paused to gather his thoughts: 'One of the oldest churches, if not the oldest church in the world, the Christian one, is perilously close to extinction in Iraq,' he said with a catch in his voice.

'And those of us who remain must be ready to face martyrdom.

We're ready for that.'

Even in late 2020, when the so called caliphate had been destroyed, several Islamic State cells still roam former Christian enclaves. Nowhere is truly safe.

Archbishop Wardar added: 'Islamic State, are the person-ification of the devil and are our tormentors. I.S confiscated our present, while seeking to wipe out our history and destroy our future.'

Archbishop Wardar is as much at home ministering to his flock in Erbil as hobnobbing with a President in the Oval Office or taking tea with Britain's Prince Charles in London - the heir to the British throne has always taken a concerned interest in the plight of Christians in the Middle East.

Although my initial impression was: this man of the cloth looks like a bit of a 'bruiser' - he's exactly the type of guy I'd want on my side in a fight!

He takes a keen interest in local and international politics and is perfectly relaxed with journalists.

It seemed a reasonable point in our conversation to ask whether the persecution of Christians in Iraq and Syria had been a challenge to his faith.

Speaking with passion, Archbishop Wardar responded, 'It's a catastrophe.

But you know, the persecution of we Christians has strengthened our faith, it's given me, personally, more courage to fight on. Christianity is a faith of forgiveness.'

So, could he pardon the jihadists who'd beheaded and committed countless other atrocities against Christian families?

Without a moment's hesitation he said, 'What kind of Christian would I be if I didn't forgive? We forgive those who murdered us, who tortured us, who raped us, who sought to destroy everything about us. We forgive them. In the name of Christ, we forgive them.'

When the Archbishop and I met, Baghdad and other big cities like Najaf and Basrah were rocked by ongoing street protests against corruption and mismanagement by the government. Hundreds of, mainly young, Iraqis had died in the violence.

Similar protests flared again in late 2020, sparked by similar grievances, although the demonstrators' violence and government crackdown had been less brutal.

Commenting, Archbishop Wardar said: 'Instead of bringing hope and prosperity, the current government structure has brought continued corruption and despair, especially to the youth of Iraq.'

He added: 'Our young people have made it clear they want Iraq to be independent of foreign interference, and to be a place where all can live together as equal citizens in a country of legitimate pluralism and respect for all.

At stake is whether Iraq will finally emerge from the trauma of Saddam, and the past sixteen years, to become a legitimate, independent and functioning country, or whether it will become a permanently lawless region, open to proxy wars between other countries and movements, and a servant to the sectarian demands of those outside Iraq.'

Archbishop Wardar was mildly optimistic.

'If protests lead to a new government with a new constitution: not based in Sharia, but instead based upon the fundamental concepts of freedom for all... then a time of hope can still exist for the long suffering Iraqi people,' he said.

When the Pope had to postpone his planned visit to Iraq in 2020 over security concerns, a Vatican spokesman sent a message to Iraq's Christians. The Pope said: 'To you citizens of Iraq, I say I am very close to you. You are in a battleground. You suffer war, from one side and the other. I pray for you and I pray for your country.'

As soon as the new date of the Pope's visit was publicised Archbishop Wardar reacted with joy by tweeting: 'I thank the Pope for his courageous decision to visit Iraq in March 2021. It has always been his mission to go to the margins and the marginalised. His important flock here is not forgotten. The Pope will come spreading the gospel of peace, goodwill and reconciliation for all in Iraq.'

And so on March 5th 2021, Pope Francis made history by becoming the first leader of the world's Catholics to visit Iraq.

I was on assignment for an African-based news channel Arise News and *The Catholic Herald* to cover the visit - one of the most difficult reporting jobs in my career due to intense security and social distancing restrictions imposed by the Covid pandemic.

Few Popes in modern times have succeeded in bringing

about fundamental change to the lives of millions. St John Paul II did. His repeated trips to Poland inspired Poles to rise up against communism and went some way to bringing about the collapse of the Iron Curtain, although it was Margaret Thatcher and Ronald Reagan who finished off the job.

So could Pope Francis cap that by rescuing Iraq's dwindling Christian population from extinction and draw Islam and Christianity together? The task he set himself was mind bogglingly profound. Christians have been persecuted in Iraq for generations including suffering genocide under the Ottomans. In recent decades it was ironically only during the reign of tyrant Saddam Hussein that followers of Jesus had an easier time of it.

Saddam's cabinet included deputy prime minister and foreign minister Tariq Aziz, who was born Mikhail Yuhanna to a Chaldean Catholic family in northern Iraq.

Anglicans fared well too under Saddam. I recall St George's in Haifa Street, Baghdad where services conducted by Canon Andrew White, the so-called, Vicar of Baghdad, were always packed.

In the town of Barzan, in the Kurdish north, there's a plaque near the grave of the father of modern day Kurdistan, Mustafa Barzani, which neatly summed up the mood of the age. It read: 'Kurdistan is a place of all religions.'

But with Saddam gone in 2003 the jihadists of Al Qaeda - and later Islamic State (ISIS) - took advantage of a power vacuum and gained a foothold in Iraq.

Jihadist attacks on Christian communities were horrific beyond belief. I well remember reporting on the bombing of a Chaldean church in the Karrada district of Baghdad in 2004 after a massive suicide truck bomb. When the cameraman and I arrived we found what was left of the congregation scattered on the street outside - limbs and bits of torsos hung on nearby telephone lines.

A decade later ISIS's campaign against all faiths other than theirs was brutal, but it was their assault on Christians that shocked the world including the wholesale desecration of churches shrines and worst of all: forcing families to convert or die.

ISIS may have been somewhat neutralised, but sickening random attacks on Christians, predominantly Chaldeans, continued in Iraq. A family of three, a doctor, his wife and mother, were stabbed to death in their home in Baghdad in March 2018.

In the same month, another Christian was shot dead in front of his house in the city and a Christian convert was killed by his father-in-law after he became aware of his conversion.

Meanwhile in 2021 there were multiple reports of Christian women in Iraq being sexually harassed and assaulted by Shia militias.

So that was the backdrop to Pope Francis's twin campaigns to reassert the presence of Christians in Iraq and bring the country's religious factions together. After visiting two churches in Baghdad, where in one -The Lady of Salvation – fifty-eight Christians died in an Al-Qaeda suicide attack in 2010 and after sitting down with the leader of Iraq's Shia Grand Ayatollah Ali Sistani in Najaf in central Iraq, the Pope ended the last full day of an historic pilgrimage to Iraq by saying mass at a football arena in Erbil before thousands of adoring Christians who'd travelled there from across the country to receive his blessing.

The Franso Harriri stadium holds 25,000 but less than half that number were able to attend the ticket only event due to social distancing rules. Many of the congregation were seated distanced on white chairs on the pitch, the remainder similarly spaced out in the stands. The Mass featured a statue of the Virgin Mary that was restored after ISIS jihadists chopped off the head and hands.

The Pope blessed the statue, which was transported from the church in Keramlis, a Christian village on the Nineveh Plains, to a place of honour on the altar at today's mass.

Keramlis, an ancient Assyrian town less than thirty kilometers southeast of Mosul, fell to Islamic State in August 2014, two months after the extremists took Mosul and surrounding areas, sending most inhabitants fleeing.

In his homily, Pope Francis preached on the divine power and wisdom in contrast with the human folly that believes itself sufficient, especially when it is powerful. 'The truth,' said Pope Francis, 'is that all of us need the power and wisdom of God revealed by Jesus on the Cross.'

'Here in Iraq,' Pope Francis went on to say: 'how many of your brothers and sisters, friends and fellow citizens bear the wounds of war and violence, wounds both visible and invisible! The temptation is to react to these and other painful experiences with human power, human wisdom.'

At the end of the mass the Pope thrilled the crowds as he did a lap of honour in the Popemobile in front of the President of the Kurdish Regional Government.

Earlier the Pope visited a region that witnessed some of the worst atrocities and destruction by ISIS jihadists after they scythed. into north Iraq from Syria.

In Mosul, where locals have a reputation for living life to the full and smiling through adversity, youngsters resplendent in their Sunday best, joined moms and dads in song and waved palm branches to give the Pope a joyous welcome amid rubble and bombed out buildings.

'Oh Lord, he's standing in the heart of Mosul,' 'Santo Padre, I can't believe my eyes!' said one Christian Tweeter.

Arguably the most powerfully symbolic moment came when the Pope led prayers in Church Square, sitting on a white chair on a raised red carpeted platform dwarfed by collapsed buildings. The cross he unveiled had been made from wood from ruined churches.

Referring to the dark days of ISIS occupation the Pope said: 'How merciless it is that this nation, the cradle of civilisation, ought to have been troubled by so barbarous a blow, with historical locations of worship destroyed and lots of hundreds of individuals – Muslims, Christians, Yazidis and others – forcibly displaced or killed.'

The Pope released a dove of peace high into the skies over Mosul and for the first time on this trip it was safe enough for him to abandon his armoured car to tour the Old City in a golf buggy see for himself the devastation wrought by ISIS and conflict which ousted them, including the ruined Syriac Catholic Al-Tahera church.

Continuing the theme of his whole mission: 'We are all brothers,' the Pope spoke today about the destruction hatred between communities brings. 'Fraternity is extra sturdy than fratricide,' he said.

The Pope would have been delighted to hear decorative gold crosses used in the Church Square ceremony were created by twenty-two-year-old sculptor Omar, one of hundreds of Muslim volunteers who've been working to restore Christian churches for more than two years.

'It's a great honour to receive the Pope here in Mosul. Different faiths must work together,' he said.

Qarakosh, thirty-five kilometers east of Mosul, was over-run by ISIS on August 6th 2014. Every family who could flee left the city, many of those who stayed and refused to convert to the jihadists' extreme version of Islam were shot or beheaded. Women and young girls were taken as sex slaves. Churches were desecrated, icons and chalices used for target practice.

The Pope travelled by helicopter across the Nineveh plains to Qarakosh to hear testimonies from families and to pray in the Church of the Immaculate Conception.

Thousands thonged the route of the motorcade which appeared more presidential in style than papal. As the Pope's armoured limousine and back up vehicles slowly wound into town a phalanx of around thirty bodyguards walked in step either side - a chill reminder that cells of Islamic State remain active within less than forty kilometers from Qarakosh and may well have sleeper cells in the city.

More doves of peace were released as crowds chanted, 'Hallelujah! Pappa Francis,' as the Pope passed by. Others who couldn't get close watched on a giant TV screen. During the church ceremony the Pope urged the Christian communities not to give up hope despite the horrors they'd endured.

He said: 'Certainly, there will be moments when faith can waiver, when it seems that God does not see or act. This was true for you in the darkest days of the war, and it is true too in these days of global health crisis and great insecurity. At times like these, remember that Jesus is by your side. Do not stop dreaming. Do not give up. Do not lose hope.'

As a further boost to the Christians of Qarakosh the Pope was able to return a sacred manuscript saved from ISIS jihadists which had been restored in Italy. The book, Sidra, written in the ancient language of Aramaic and dating to the 14th and 15th century, was one of the oldest books in the Church of the Immaculate Conception, and was saved by local priests. It contains liturgical prayers for Easter services.

In terms of numbers the Pope has attracted the biggest crowds so far in this trip, partly because there are far more Christians in the north of Iraq which is now home to thousands who've sought sanctuary there. And the semi-autonomous Kurdish Government has also given sanctuary to Christians fleeing on-going fighting in Syria.

As the Pope flew back to Rome the following day it was time to assess - was the trip a success?

And on paper it looks good for his legacy.

But Iraq is a maddeningly, unpredictable place, a witches' brew of political and religious factions constantly vying for power and with a population in revolt.

The so-called October Revolution which began in 2019, when the youth of Iraq rose up against rampant government corruption and unemployment, has not gone away and is still bubbling in cities like Nasiriyah. If elections do go ahead in late 2021 there could well be a change of government And the Pope may have established a working relationship with Grand Ayatollah Sistani, but he's ninety with a heart condition and no one is sure who his replacement will be.

Meanwhile Iran remains the dominant outside force in Iraq

and senior Shia clerics including the Islamic Republic's spiritual leader Ayatollah Ali Khameni will be chewing the carpet over the Pope's meeting with Sistani, which implies the latter is superior to Khameni.

Media in Iran, which is effectively state controlled, covered Pope Francis's visit with a mixture of cautious factual reporting devoid of opinion and analysis, most conservative papers ignored it all together. So now it's likely Teheran will begin to undo the good work Sistani and Pope Francis have achieved - that's the harsh reality of the fractious Middle East.

Bringing about change in Iraq is always a long term project and only years from now - perhaps after Francis has left us - will we know whether the pilgrim Pope's tricky visit to Iraq was worth the risk.

9. 'Please help me!'

My fixer Karokh and I were finding our bearings at a refugee camp at Bardarash, twenty five miles north of Mosul. The purpose of us being there was to hear testimony from Kurds who'd escaped the horrors of civil war in Syria.

I noticed an elderly man striding purposefully towards me.

His dark eyes held me in a steady stare; he looked deranged and for some moments, I thought he meant me harm.

He stopped abruptly about one pace from me; his face coated in dust and grime, his eyes hollow and cheeks sunken.

A light breeze blew wisps of his unkempt, iron-grey hair across his forehead as we stood nose-to-nose for a couple of silent seconds.

'You are Englishman?' he suddenly blurted.

I confirmed I was.

'Please help me... please Englishman, I don't know where I am.'

When journalists pitch up at Kurdish refugee camps we and our photographers' lenses are often drawn to children - Syrian kids are especially photogenic - but of course victims of Syria's civil war are people of all ages and differing mental and physical states.

The elderly Syrian Kurd, who begged for my help, was a sharp reminder to me that older folk were also caught in the nightmare and arguably suffered more distress than youngsters who, from my observations, adapted remarkably quickly to the deprivations caused by war.

I'd spent time in north Syria before the civil war and was familiar with the rural villages the old man had fled from.

Families in Kurdish farming communities lead simple lives: raising children, working the land, perhaps growing wheat, tomatoes or cotton, or tending a few chickens in small holdings.

They get up with sun and go to bed when it gets dark.

Life is simple and taken at a slow pace. Any excitement, or breaks from the humdrum, are usually connected to the immediate family like: weddings, funerals or celebrations like the Nowruz holiday.

The old man told me his name was Alwan, he was a part time teacher and his normally serene world had been shattered when a mob of killers stormed his sleepy village one morning.

He told me his sons, their wives, his daughters and his grand-children had all been murdered, although it wasn't entirely clear which militia group had carried out the massacre.

In his confused state he couldn't tell me whether they'd been shot to death by Islamic State jihadis or any number of other militias; perhaps they were Syrian, Turkish or Russian.

It was academic anyway. His family was gone and that was the end of it. He mourned alone and had found solace in telling a total stranger like me what had happened.

All I could do was listen.

He went on to explain he'd paid traffickers all his savings of around US$300 to smuggle him across the border from north Syria into Iraqi Kurdistan.

He told me he'd arrived at the Bardarash Camp the night before and had no possessions other than the clothes he was wearing.

He said he was very hungry and needed water. I had a bottle, which I gladly handed him.

But that was as much as I could practically do to help Alwan and I gently led him by the hand to a French charity's aid tent and explained to the young team that the old man needed help.

I said my goodbyes, shook his bony hand and walked away; his eyes followed me, but there was little else I could do.

I felt utterly useless.

I learned from aid workers that Syrian Kurdish refugees had been arriving at the camp at the rate of a 1000 a day. Bardarash held 11,292, it was already full to capacity and they could take no more.

By chance, Alwan had been one of the last to be allowed in.

I've visited other refugee camps in Kurdistan. Bardarash was much the same. Thousands of white canvas tents, with logos like UNHCR, cover vast swathes of desert scrubland as far as the eye could see. Most times they are laid out like a small American town with a central dirt road down the middle, with parallel lanes and cross streets. Marquees are used as schools and shops and most have an awful sense of permanence.

In the Middle East paperwork is king and as I walked around Bardarash I noticed families tramping back and forth between one charity office and another, clutching flimsy chitties.

They were searching for Kurdish officials to stamp their bits of paper so they could access medical care or food rations, like bread or perhaps a plate of rice and lamb stew.

Every refugee I spoke to had a disturbing story.

Young Dilawar, aged thirteen, had lost his parents when Turkish gunmen stormed his small town and started shooting at random.

'I cried out for my mother and father,' he told me, through an interpreter.

'But, it was dark. I accidentally let go of my mother's hand and both she and my father were lost in the crowds. I looked and looked, and I'm sure they searched for me, but nothing. As I'd lost my parents, I joined others from my village and ended up here.'

A mother called Sihan beckoned Karokh and I to step inside her canvas home for a cup of sweet tea. Sihan explained she was from Kobane and had arrived at the camp with her three sons and two daughters, aged between two and fourteen.

She said her husband had stayed behind in Syria to guard the family home against looters.

'When we hugged and said goodbye, neither of us knew whether we'd see each other again. I don't know whether my husband's dead or alive,' she said.

Sihan and I talked about former US President Donald Trump's decision to withdraw support for Kurdish fighters in north Syria.

'Our fighters spilled blood with the Americans,' Sihan said 'And then they go and desert us; Trump left the Kurds to be blown to pieces. Believe me the Kurds will turn on the Americans for doing that. Kurds are trusting people but we don't know who to trust anymore; not the Turks or the Russians and definitely not the US.'

Most of the refugees I met had arrived in the previous two or three weeks of fighting and they all spoke of their hopes of finding work in cities like Erbil, or returning home once it was safe.

They didn't seem to be aware Bardarash camp was likely their home for the foreseeable future, probably months or even years, and they couldn't work legally in Kurdistan. The chances of returning to war ravaged Syria was next to impossible.

Alessandra Sacchetti, Programme Manager in Mosul for the aid group *Action contra la Faim* told me: 'The families we've taken in are in a honeymoon period right now.

They're happy... euphoric even, because they're in a place of safety, having escaped the death and destruction. At some point, they'll want to leave the camp - but, they can't just walk out. The Kurdish authorities don't want thousands of people wandering the countryside. It's very sad but most will have to stay here, for many months. They can't leave. I'm not sure they understand that.'

I discovered from aid workers there was another stumbling block for the refugees with hopes of returning home. The Al-Assad regime in Damascus had imposed strict conditions on anyone returning to Syria, including being positively vetted by various Syrian security agencies.

One refugee showed me a document every person aged between eighteen and fifty five had to fill in and sign before they'd be allowed back into Syria. The sections to be completed were:

Applicant's Name and Surname: Father name and surname: Mother name and surname: Date of birth: Place and number of register: National ID number: Previous address: Current address: Cell phone number: Landline number: Brief of your life: Political orientation: Current job: Previous job: Sentences and arrests: Have you ever raised a gun against the Syrian Army? Have you ever committed a crime against innocent civilians or had blood on your hands? Have you travelled outside the country?

Do you have any relatives detained during the current events?
Date: --/--/2019 Name and signature: Left thumb fingerprint.

All of this information had to be cross-checked with every Syrian security agency before a refugee's return was approved, a process that would take months in normal times, and forever in times of war.

How the Kurdish refugees I met got through winter under canvas I can only wonder about because it was especially cold in Iraq where, in 2020, it snowed for the first time in fifteen years.

As I look at my notes now, I want to know what happened to Fayak, aged twenty-four with his wife and two children. They talked to me in the camp about going home and were preparing to pay people smugglers.

But, did they make it back across the border safely and what did they find? Was their house still standing? Were the elderly relatives they had to leave behind still alive?

And as I write this book in the warm comfort of my London apartment I can only hope Alwan, the old man who was so confused and distressed, got the help and support he desperately needed. Was he even alive?

We journalists have to stand back and not become involved in the story, but it doesn't mean we don't care deeply about the people we write about.

Young Syrian Kurdish refugees

Bardarash refugee camp

10. Brown envelope anyone?

I'd like to talk about one of the oldest of Mesopotamian traditions; a leaden cliché in that part of the world.

Brown envelopes stuffed with greenbacks; millions of dollars syphoned into secret London bank accounts; couriers slipping through airport VIP lounges with gold ingots sewn in overcoat linings. Yes, Iraq is truly one of the most corrupt nations on the planet.

In 2020 Transparency International ranked Iraq 168th on the corruption scale out of a list of 180 - as bad as Afghanistan, Libya, Sudan and Venezuela, although not as crooked as bottom of the table Somalia.

Iraqis grumble, but they accept soft corruption as a routine; a lubrication of the wheels if you like.

Let's take something as mundane as obtaining a driving licence.

An applicant won't even get inside a government run licence office without shoving a few dinars into the hands of the poorly paid man on the gate. And when the paperwork and stamping is done, the driving licence won't be handed over until the desk clerk has been slipped a 'sweetener'.

Take education: if Iraqi parents want their kid enrolled in a decent school they have to grease the headmaster's palm. It's an unwritten law. The same goes for medical care. The more greenbacks you slip the doctor, the more likely you, or your relative, will live to see old age.

Kurdish friends may wish to correct me but I should say I haven't come across this kind of low level corruption in the Kurdish north. You can't bribe Kurdish traffic cops with a handful of dinars, or a pack of cigarettes, as you so easily can further south in Baghdad or Basrah.

But Iraq, including Kurdistan, is also weighed down by corruption on an industrial scale involving those at the very top of government. In 2018 the Saudi Arabian owned *Al-Watan* newspaper reported that between them, ministers in Baghdad and Erbil syphoned off US $200 billion in bribes every year.

The publication also reported most of it had been laundered and converted into real estate in cities like London and New York or into liquid funds.

The same newspaper claimed one senior veteran Kurdish politician held US$48 billion worth of bonds, real estate, and investments in Swiss, German, and Italian companies.

I can add some evidence of my own.

In 2013, I took a short break from journalism to work for an organisation liaising between potential Western corporate investors and Iraqi government ministries. I found myself in a meeting in Erbil where a Kurdish minister was negotiating with a Western corporation over a huge infrastructure project worth millions.

After the usual round of sweet teas and pleasantries, the minister suddenly removed his glasses, put his pen and paperwork down, and leant across the table.

'So gentlemen, what's my commission... as consultant? Should we say... ten per cent?'

His eyes widened, expectantly.

I was shocked. Not because the old rogue had demanded a pay-off amounting to millions of bucks, but because he'd asked for it openly, in front of junior staff, and without any sense of shame.

In short, it was the normalcy of it, which took me aback.

I should add: the directors of the Western firm bidding for the contract weren't prepared to risk being caught by their own country's bribery laws and pulled out of any deal. A Turkish outfit picked the contract up instead, presumably having agreed to pay the politician a massive bung.

Corruption at the Kurdish Ministry of Natural Resources (effectively the oil ministry) has been well publicised in media reports.

After Ashti Hawrami was appointed minister in 2006, foreign oil and gas exploration companies made no secret they had to 'pay to play'.

Oilprice.com reported: 'His (Hawrami) usual cut was between twenty to thirty per cent of the overall value of the deal up front, with extra payments along the way, as various milestones on production are passed, and lesser payments were to be made to other senior figures in the administration.'

When he was appointed, this twenty to thirty per cent was passed off as 'going to an account that would be used for the benefit of the Kurdish people,' but this pretence seems to have been dropped now.

Allegations about corruption in the Kurdish oil ministry continued through all Hawrami's terms in office.

In 2015, he was the subject of a parliamentary investigation in South Korea over claims that a US$31 million signature bonus, as part of a 2008 Korea National Oil Corporation contract, was a bribe to Hawrami.

When the Russian oil giant Rosneft began oil exploration in Kurdistan in 2017, it reportedly paid an eye-watering US$250 million to an 'unnamed Kurdish government official' in 'consultancy fees'.

And in August 2019, in a lawsuit against Hawrami, the plaintiff, Dynasty Petroleum, claimed it was the subject of Kurdish government harassment from 2014 onwards, after it refused to pay a bribe.

Meanwhile, Hawrami's estranged, former wife Chrakhan Rafik, who was sentenced by an Erbil court to four years for fraud, and survived what she claimed was an assassination attempt in Paris in 2019, wrote to the then President Masoud Barzani a letter which began:

You are being looted and oppressed by corrupted hands.
Dear citizens, I would like to say without a doubt that the Minister of Natural Resources (Hawrami) and his band have seized hundreds of millions of dollars and smuggled them abroad at a time when the people of Kurdistan Region are in need of a meal for them and their children.

Ashti Hawrami stepped down from his ministerial role in 2019, to be replaced in January 2021 by Kamal Al-Atroshi, but he remains a Cabinet adviser.

During my last visit to Kurdistan, I met with a former senior Kurdish government minister and talk turned to corruption.

I put evidence to him from a Wikileaks report that showed almost all major infrastructure projects in Erbil had been carried out by eight conglomerates: Diyar Group, Eagle, Falcon, KAR, Nasri, Sandi, Silver Star and Ster, all of which had what were described as 'close ties' to the ruling Barzani family.

Coincidentally, the day I met the former minister, America's Variety magazine reported the ruling Barzani family had spent almost US$50 million on two homes in Beverley Hills, one a few blocks from Rodeo Drive. Reporter James McLean described one as:

A colossal structure which utterly obliterates its neighbours in sheer size alone.

Within the mega-mansion's nearly 21,000 square feet of gilt-trimmed living space are a beauty salon, elevator, indoor basketball court, 17 bathrooms and even a bowling alley.

The McLean article went on:

And from the street, the European-influenced architecture invokes Versailles, its towering limestone face festooned with a bonanza of Corinthian columns, intricate moldings and decorative quoins. The house looks like money – a remarkably showy sort of money.

The Barzanis strongly denied the story.

The former minister smiled, 'No one believes the denial.'

He added, 'Look, it works like this... When a shopping mall or new hospital is given the go ahead by the Government, a construction company no one's ever heard of appears from nowhere and lands the big contract. You usually find the mystery corporation is run by relatives of members of the ruling parties, like the Barzanis.'

It's a simple as that.

'It's the way business is done in Kurdistan. These days the pay-off to the minister and his officials is usually built into the contract, rather than a straight bribe.'

The Kurdish public has long wearied of graft at a high level. Thousands took to the streets in 2017 and again in 2019 and 2020, to protest at government corruption.

'Yes, we've seen demonstrations about corruption, but mass protest isn't likely,' the former minister told me.

'That's because the corrupt system, as bad as it is, has resulted in the construction of highways, shopping malls, cinema complexes, hotels and apartment blocks. Kurds are not complaining, they're enjoying it.

It's that benign element to corruption - graft with a heart, if you like; a dark kind of win-win, which keeps a lid on things.'

The Gorran political party campaigns on an anti-corruption platform and I met a senior figure, Hoshayar Omar in Sulaimaniyah, a city with a spectacular building programme of shopping malls and high-end hotels, most of which were linked to corruption.

'The leaders of the two main political parties the PUK and the KDP are like mafia dons. Their tentacles reach everywhere and this is fuelling endless corruption on a massive scale,' said Hoshayar.

'They run their own internal security apparatus, their own armies, the courts are in their pockets, so they'll never be prosecuted.'

I asked him: what happens to all millions paid in bribes and 'commissions'?

'Ministers and their officials usually have dual nationality. That allows them to syphon billions into foreign banks accounts to buy opulent apartments and mansions in cities like London. Once the money's been laundered it's untraceable.'

Hoshayar and I agreed Iraqi Kurdistan's politicians were never going to be prosecuted, tried and sent to jail.

So what was his solution?

'The Kurdistan economy is centred on oil which the ruling families control and pays for all the shopping malls, apartment complexes and sports stadia we've seen springing up,' Hoshayar said.

'To beat this system of endemic corruption we need to see diversification away from oil to other sources of income like agriculture, mining of precious minerals and tourism. We also need to empower parliament to be able to scrutinise contracts more and prevent kick-backs to the ruling elite.'

'Until then, the ruling classes will continue to line their pockets,' he added.

To the credit of the Kurdish media, which is broadly in the pocket of the ruling parties and individual politicians, corruption in high places is often the subject of local newspaper investigations, radio phone-ins and tv chat shows.

And recently, Prime Minister Masrour Barzani has been making noises about cracking down on graft, giving Kurds hope things might change.

When I was last in Kurdistan Barzani told a conference in Doha, 'We have stopped corruption. Nobody can rely on a friend of a friend to get things done anymore.'

And speaking at the Middle East Research Institute he made a further pledge, 'I am committed to fight corruption; not only financial corruption, but corruption in all forms.'

When I sat down with a senior British diplomat in Erbil for an informal briefing, he reckoned that if the Kurdish government didn't get a grip on corruption, there could be serious civil unrest in the years ahead.

'Running a corrupt economy is all very well for the upper strata of society,' he said. 'But without a strategy for looking after the poorest in society, the rulers of Kurdistan are asking for trouble in the long term.'

To end my investigation into corruption I spent an afternoon on line trying to discover if any senior Kurdish politician or official had been prosecuted for high-level corruption in recent years. I found no evidence.

The KRG's recently appointed Parliamentary Speaker Rewaz Fayeq Hussein sighed, 'Only one or two small fish have been caught. None of the big ones.'

President Nechirvan Barzani

Mustapha Barzani

11. Chalabi the Cheshire Cat

When I was last in Kurdistan in late 2019 and pre-Covid, the Iraqi capital, Baghdad was in turmoil; rocked by bloody protests over corruption and government incompetence.

After breakfast one morning, I switched on the television news to learn Iraq's President, Barham Saleh, a Kurd, had left Baghdad quite suddenly and turned up in Erbil where he has a home.

I was puzzled. Why would the Iraqi leader leave Baghdad at the peak of a crisis?

I rang my best contacts and learned Saleh had received serious death threats – not from protest leaders, but from members of his own cabinet.

He returned to Baghdad some days later.

Like several of the current generation of Iraqi leaders Saleh had spent time in jail under Saddam's regime where he was tortured before he eventually escaped and found sanctuary in the UK.

He's a highly intelligent, quietly spoken man of letters with a bachelor's degree in engineering from Cardiff University and a doctorate in statistics and computer applications from the University of Liverpool.

Although having an engineering and statistics background, politics was always his life and he was one of the founders of the Patriotic Union of Kurdistan, the PUK party, one of north Iraq's ruling duopoly.

Before he became President of Iraq he was the Kurdish Government's Prime Minister.

I've had the pleasure of meeting Saleh a number of times.

In 2012 I was invited to an informal dinner party with Saleh and his family in the salubrious surroundings of Saludhin, a mountain enclave, a thirty-minute drive from Erbil, where the President of Kurdistan, his close family and associates also maintain mansions and palaces.

Chatting with Saleh over dinner about his exploits in the Kurdish resistance was memorable, not only for the thrilling and agreeable conversation, but also for the unexpected appearance at the *soiree* by one of the most colourful characters in Iraqi politics: Ahmed Chalabi.

Although Chalabi was a Shia Arab, born in Baghdad, he had strong family connections to Iraqi Kurdistan - an honorary Kurd, so to speak.

Chalabi was also highly intelligent, charismatic, with a PhD in mathematics.

We journalists knew him as a stylish, media friendly, personality, always immaculately dressed with a permanent Cheshire Cat smile.

Before entering Iraqi politics he'd been a savvy businessman and had amassed a fortune of at least US$100 million.

Famously, in 1992, he was accused of embezzling millions of dollars from the Petra Bank in Jordan, an institution he'd helped to set up. He strongly denied cooking the books and syphoning off a fortune, but he was tried in his absence and sentenced by a Jordanian court to twenty-two years in jail on thirty-one charges of fraud, theft, misuse of depositor funds and currency speculation.

His jail sentence wasn't upheld, and he was eventually pardoned by Jordan's King Abdullah.

Whether he was corrupt, we'll never know and frankly, Middle Eastern businessmen and politicians are renowned for having their hands in till. It's expected and reluctantly tolerated.

What no one can deny: Chalabi played a key role in shaping modern day Iraq.

His influence started when he led an exiles' pressure group: the Iraqi National Congress (INC) including Iraqi Kurdistan's PUK and KDP parties, which, from 1997 onwards, lobbied the US Congress to support the overthrow of Saddam Hussein.

After 9/11, Chalabi's INC group began supplying intelligence reports to US officials, including alleged evidence Saddam had weapons of mass destruction.

The claims turned out to be untrue, but it was accepted by the Bush administration which used it as a casus belli for the US-led invasion of Iraq in 2003, changing the course of Iraqi history.

After Saddam was overthrown I did several television interviews with Chalabi in Iraq; one in 2005, when I was a correspondent for Fox News, being the most memorable.

I'd arranged to sit down with him at his home in the upmarket district of Al-Khadimiya, in north Baghdad.

Suicide bombers and kidnappings were a daily occurrence in the capital, and neighbourhoods like Al-Khadimiya always crackled with tensions.

I was uneasy about the timing of the interview; Chalabi was only free mid-evening and in Baghdad bad things happened after dark.

However, Fox News had provided cameraman Mike and I

with robust security: former British SAS soldiers and US Navy Seals. So, we decided to take the risk of visiting Chalabi in Al-Khadimiya after nightfall.

Chalabi's villa was in a street lined with opulent homes – one a pastiche of the White House.

Each home had a gaggle of security men hanging around the front gates; gum-chewing young men who took their cue from Hollywood: dark shades, shiny lounge-suits and hair gelled into spikes.

One or two chatted into their sleeves and as well as toting AK 47s you could see from the bulge in their coat jackets they also packed handguns.

We pulled up close to Chalabi's house and left our own security detail to wait for us in the street whilst we marched up to the front door where our host's own 'goons' seemed overly nervous, for no obvious reason.

After being frisked robustly, and having had our camera gear taken apart and reassembled, we were given the all clear.

I knocked on the front door.

It was opened by the man of the house who welcomed cameraman Mike and I like old friends.

Chalabi loved appearing on television and his ensemble that evening included an expensive looking sports-jacket, a flamboyant, yellow floral tie and matching pocket handkerchief.

As we shook hands I could see he'd already applied anti-shine foundation on his face cheeks and forehead; a sign of a seasoned television professional.

Cameraman Mike set up two chairs for the interview.

I sat opposite Chalabi, who had his back to French windows, beyond which was an extensive garden with cactuses and palms.

I bowled the old fox a couple of soft-ball questions about his recent visit to the US and I was about ask him about claims he was a CIA asset, when there was unmistakable crack from a handgun, followed by another... and another.

From my front row seat I could see and hear men in black as they leapt between palm trees in Chalabi's garden shooting at each other like something out of the Wild West.

Chalabi had his back to the action and heard the gunfire but, cool as cucumber, he continued chatting to me on camera as if nothing out of the ordinary was happening.

Aware my viewers would expect an explanation about the mayhem behind his right shoulder, I interrupted Chalabi's conversational flow with: 'Sir, I think we should pause this interview.'

'There's a gun fight in your garden.'

With a nonchalant wave of his hand and without turning around to look, he said: 'Yes, it sounds like it.'

'Don't worry. My boys will sort it out.'

He continued: 'Go on Cookson, what were you saying about the CIA?'

Chalabi's instinct was right. In less than a minute, the crackle of gunfire had died and by the time he and I finished the interview the garden was quiet.

Afterwards, Chalabi, cameraman Mike and I put our heads out of the French windows.

It was all very normal. If there'd been any bodies or wounded in the shrubbery, they'd been hauled away. Nothing to see here!

'You see, I told you,' said a smiling Chalabi, who patted me on the shoulder.

'My boys sorted it!'

As we packed away the camera gear I thanked Chalabi for his time and although he issued an invitation to stay for dinner, cameraman Mike and I agreed return to the Fox News compound asap.

There'd been several previous attempts on Chalibi's life. Had we just witnessed another?

I never found out.

The last time I saw Chalabi was in early 2015. I was strapped in my seat on an Iraqi Airways flight from Sulaimaniyah to Baghdad.

There wasn't a spare seat and the plane was ready to leave, but we were held up for some reason.

A stewardess whispered to me they were waiting for 'a V.VIP'.

A full hour passed, and just as we passengers were getting very restless on a hot afternoon in a sweltering plane that was going nowhere, there was a flurry of activity.

A couple of black limos swept across the airport apron, and who should leap out of one car and bound up the aircraft steps?

An out-of-breath Chalabi.

The airline had held the plane all that time, just for him. But there wasn't a free seat for the newly arrived V.VIP.

Quick as a flash, a stewardess indicated he should turn left and sit in the cockpit jump-seat behind the pilot and first officer.

As he disappeared into the cockpit, Chalabi, ever the show-man, flashed a smile and a cheery wave to us lesser mortals in the main cabin. It was pure showbiz.

And we passengers waved back; some even broke into appreciative applause.

Ahmed Chalabi, former Iraqi Deputy Prime Minister, ex Oil Minister, died from heart failure in Baghdad on November 3rd 2015, aged 71.

Iraqi politics had lost one of its most enigmatic and influential characters.

12. Jalal Talabani

Modern Kurdish politics is a mess of petty rivalries and corruption. It was ever thus.

The two main political parties the KDP and the PUK - or as I like to call them: Tweedledum and Tweedledee - have been at loggerheads since the latter, a breakaway movement, was founded in 1975.

The KDP - the big tent nationalist party - had been formed in 1946 in Mahabad, Iran, about which there's more in chapter thirty-seven.

At the time of writing, relations were cordial, rather than warm, but at least they weren't on the verge of a hot war, such as the one they fought against each other between May 1994 and November 1997.

Richard Spencer, of the UK's Daily Telegraph, wrote this about ongoing political infighting in north Iraq:

Try selling editors in London stories about the war between the two largest Kurdish factions in Iraq, the Kurdistan Democratic Party (KDP) and the Patriotic Union of Kurdistan (PUK), or about the ideological battle between the pro-Western, capitalist KDP and the Marxist PKK, and you could hear the blood draining from their faces.

Kurdish politics is definitely missing its traditional peace-maker, political veteran Mr Jalal Talabani who could always smooth things over.

After a lifetime in politics he suffered a major stroke in 2012 and was back and forth to hospital in Germany for years, until he died in Berlin from a brain hemorrhage in October 2017 aged 83.

Talabani was a hugely likable character who helped form the PUK movement during a coffee shop huddle with a handful of other hard-left activists in 1975 in the Syrian capital Damascus.

He steered the party through good times and bad and stayed very much in control even as he served as Iraqi President from 2005 - the first non-Arab to hold the post.

I liked genial Talabani and during assignments I joined him, when I could, at his office in Sulaimaniyah for invaluable off the record chats.

He'd dispense vast quantities Scotch, lean back in his leather chair, puff on a Havana, put his feet up on his desk and then gossip away about the indiscretions of political rivals. Occasionally he roared with laughter at the madness of it all.

But he's gone now and without his benign influence the ruling PUK and KDP parties seem to be constantly at loggerheads.

Hopes rose of a massive shake up to the Kurdish political system when Nawshirwan Mustafa established the anti-corruption Gorran party in 2009, which was potentially a huge challenge to the two main parties.

It was not to be. Mustafa died in his hometown of Sulaimaniyah in May 2017, thought to be from pneumonia.

And under the new leadership of Omar Said Ali, the party has failed to present a lasting challenge to the KDP and PUK. Gorran won just twelve seats in the 2018 Kurdistan parliamentary election - down from twenty five and claimed only five seats in the 2018 Iraqi parliamentary elections.

Rocked by claims of nepotism and corruption, yes corruption! the Gorran movement's popularity is still in decline in 2020.

So Tweedledum and Tweedledee are once again, effectively without serious political challenge.

13. A matter of 'honour'?

In a sophisticated society such as Kurdistan, it's always astonished me so called 'honour killings' are still perpetrated and broadly tolerated by a large proportion of the population.

Victims are buried in fenced off areas such as in the cemetery I saw in Kaznasa, Erbil, where women - and some men - lay in unmarked graves separated from the rest, forgotten and unmourned in death.

In Kurdish society, as elsewhere in the Middle East, maintenance of a woman's virginity and her sexual purity is considered the responsibility of a male relative, for example: her father, brothers or male cousins.

A woman is at risk of being killed for bringing shame on her family if she's actually committed a so called 'honour offence,' or perceived to have. This can include: marriage, friendships that are viewed as 'inappropriate,' being the victim or rape or kidnapping and even 'inappropriate' dress.

There are legal or constitutional protections for women, but because of the power of tribes and the sympathetic attitude of the courts, 'honour killings,' often go unpunished.

To get an idea of the sheer scale of the horror story I consulted the Erbil based General Directorate of Combating Violence Against Women. It reported in 2018 forty-eight Kurdish women were murdered by a male family member; that's almost one a week. That figure is probably an underestimate.

The NGO also revealed a further seventy-three Kurdish

women committed suicide that year after being accused of an 'honour' crime, some by setting themselves on fire.

Not all the women died from self-immolation. One hundred and twenty-five survived with appalling injuries and were treated at a special burns unit specially set up at a hospital in Sulaimaniyah for such cases.

The Directorate also revealed a hundred and thirteen women were sexually assaulted and it received almost ten thousand complaints of gender-based violence in 2018.

As recently as November 2020 three men were arrested on suspicion of hanging their sister to death.

The body of the woman, born in 1994 and named by police only by the initials M.A.M. was found hanging in her own home in the district of Kalar.

Police said the three brothers had already confessed, prompting the Deputy Prime Minister of the Kurdistan Region, Qubad Talabani to express his outrage over the murder via Twitter:

'We will not tolerate or accept violence against women in the name of honour – those responsible will pay a heavy price for their crime.'

14. Shayan

One of Iraqi Kurdistan's successes has been the liberation of women from the traditional shadows through public life.

Typical would be Judge Nigar Agha, first member of Erbil's judiciary in 2010 and Iraq's first Court of Appeal female member.

The Kurdish Parliament has a quota of thirty percent female members, the current Speaker of the Kurdish Parliament is the second woman in succession to hold that post, the leadership of the main political parties include women, and there are female cabinet ministers and envoys abroad, the most prominent overseas diplomat being the formidable Bayan Sami Abdul Rahman, the Kurdish Government's representative in Washington DC.

And yet, despite great strides forward, in many homes Kurdish women remain second-class citizens closeted indoors, cooking and raising children, especially in rural areas.

Overall, stark inequalities between men and women are rife.

In one everyday example: although polygamy isn't legal a Kurdish man can travel south, marry two or three times over and bring all his wives back north to Kurdistan.

To probe the standing of women and female rights in Kurdistan, I met with one of the most famous female politicians in northern Iraq: thirty-nine-year-old, Dr Shayan Askeri, who was a YouTube star before she became a Member of Parliament.

She sprang to fame in March 2018 after she joined thousands

of protestors demonstrating outside the Kurdish Parliament building in Erbil, over unpaid wages and corruption.

Shayan was owed money herself. Her modest oncologist's salary of US$1,200 a month had been cut by two thirds in an ongoing funding dispute between the Baghdad government and Kurdish regime.

She filmed the noisy demonstration on her cellphone and was still videoing when she claimed two men from the Kurdish security service verbally abused her and knocked her phone out of her hand.

She retrieved the phone and put the footage on social media, where it went viral.

Overnight, Shayan became a heroine, especially after she began giving media interviews about institutionalised corruption in Kurdistan's health service, confirming what everyone suspected already: Kurdish hospital managers and ministers were receiving financial kick-backs on medical equipment and drugs contracts.

Going public came with consequences. She said she was approached by two rank and file KDP party members days later and ordered to join the party, or get out of Kurdistan and live in exile.

She claimed they also threatened her family.

'I was outraged,' said Shayan.

'So, I joined the Gorran Party, because it stood against corruption - and I got myself elected. Now as an MP, I'm lucky to be able to fight corruption from the inside and for women's rights.'

I raised the question of so-called honour killings.

'Kurdish men simply have to change, and stop taking part

in honour killings,' said Shayan.

'Women can't change, but the men's attitude must. I'm working towards the outlawing of honour killings.'

I raised the disturbing statistic that at least one woman a week was being murdered.

'The figures are shocking,' she agreed.

'There's no justification for violence against women and, indeed, the Islamic faith forbids 'honour' killing. The Koran says all life is precious. Men need to understand that.'

Shayan also revealed a new and disturbing development involving social media.

She told me Kurdish men tricked young women and girls into sending explicit photographs of themselves. They then faced the threat of being blackmailed into having sex. In such circumstances young females were committing suicide, rather than bring shame on their family.

'Use of social media is actually resulting in murder and that has to stop,' said Shayan.

It didn't surprise me when Shayan told me she was trolled every day on Twitter and other social media outlets. She said she'd been threatened with rape and bombarded by men sending her nude photos of themselves; the latter something she'd managed to laugh off.

Adjusting her shocking pink headscarf and smiling, she said: 'John, I think I've seen everything!'

I didn't ask for more detail.

As I was getting up to leave Shayan reminded me of what she thought was her deal with destiny to fight government corruption, even though her personal safety had been threatened.

'I've been warned off by other MPs, but I will continue. It's my mission in life, I can't stop, even though they might kill me,' she pledged.

I told Shayan I thought her courage was similar to that of former Pakistani Prime Minister Benazir Bhutto whose 'life mission,' had been to champion secular rule in Pakistan.

Like Shayan, Bhutto told me in television interviews she was aware she might be assassinated, as indeed happened on December 27th 2007 in Rawalpindi, Pakistan.

Shayan paused for a moment and then said with a smile, 'Thanks for comparing me with Benazir Bhutto! But, corrupt people aren't going to stop me. However in view of what you just said, maybe I should fight my campaign a little more softly, softly.'

I told her I thought it a good idea.

Brave women like Shayan have a long struggle ahead to fight endemic corruption and improve the lot of Kurdish women, meanwhile they make amazing role models for the girls who will surely follow their footsteps in the decades ahead.

15. Those who die first

The Kurdish militia known as the *peshmerga* - fondly referred to as *the pesh* - are part of the region's DNA.

Technically, every Iraqi Kurd of fighting age - male or female - is a member. Those actually in uniform number anywhere between 80,000 and 240,000. The exact figure has always been unclear.

Historically, they've had a single primary role: to protect the Kurdish homeland.

That's meant battling against powerful armies including: the British after World War One in 1919, Iranian forces in 1946/7, Saddam Hussein's military during the 1970s and 1980s and Islamic State jihadists in the 21st century; the latter, being an ongoing conflict.

On the occasions I've been embedded as a journalist with *peshmerga* forces I've found them massively strong on commitment, camaraderie, and battlefield expertise, but ill-equipped militarily for fighting a modern war.

I made a film for the Al Jazeera news channel with the movement's elite special forces. They'd run low on ammunition and struggled with sixty-year-old Soviet-era tanks which were always getting stuck in the mud and belched clouds of choking exhaust smoke.

Peshmerga pay is relatively poor. The average foot soldier earns just 650,000 Iraqi Dinars (US$560) (335 British pounds) a month, so many have second jobs.

Although they have a generic name, they're not a united force. Not only do the main Kurdish political parties run their own units, some are aligned to individual politicians, as a sort of private army.

On my car journey to meet a member of the *pesh* top brass in an Erbil suburb, I used the time to refresh my memory on history.

To source *peshmerga* origins you need to turn the clock back 1,500 years when an elite fighting force emerged out of the Sassanian Empire. They were cavalrymen who, for the first time in ancient history, were draped head-to-toe in chain-mail armour, as were their horses. Their role was to punch through opposing infantry lines at the start of battle.

Such was their outstanding battleground successes, their armour and fighting prowess were copied by Christian Crusaders and medieval knights centuries later.

But a front-line role came at a price. Being in the first wave of any attack, life expectancy was low. That's how they got their name.

In Middle Persian *peshmerga* translates as: 'those who die first'.

I was shown into the office of intelligence chief Major-General Bahat Taymis Selki.

He was in his fifties, a gently spoken and straight talking military man, in charge of training *peshmerga* forces defending Kurdish communities in northern Syria - a key role.

When Selki and I met, there was debate amongst Kurdish politicians about merging *peshmerga* divisions into one - although to my knowledge they'd been talking about unification for years.

He was firmly in favour.

'In my view, I think the time has come for the Kurdish region to have one well-funded army,' he said.

'These days we need a strong unified militia. One *pesh* force will cut out all the in-fighting and rivalries. A single force would also help solve the problem of us being under-equipped. There'd be more to spend on buying the latest weaponry.'

I turned to events in August 2014, when Islamic State fighters came within hours of launching an assault on the *de facto* Kurdish capital, Erbil as a prelude to sweeping across the whole of north Iraq.

At the time the jihadists seemed unstoppable and before arriving at the gates of Erbil they'd had already grabbed two major tranches of territory that had once been under *peshmerga* control.

The first had been the strategically important Mosul Dam on the River Tigris north west of Mosul itself. The jihadists had threatened to blow the water barrier up. Tens of thousands would have drowned and Baghdad would have been left under fifteen feet of water.

And on a second battle front, the jihadists had swept into Sinjar province, where they ordered families to renounce their Yazidi faith or be killed.

At least 5,000 Yazidi men were shot dead or beheaded by Islamic State fighters. 7,000 Yazidi women were captured as sex-slaves. Yazidi survivors had criticised the *peshmerga* for not protecting them.

A thirty-one-year-old, called Firas told the Reuters news agency, he felt betrayed: We used to feel safe, and that the peshmerga had our back. We trusted the peshmerga, but they withdrew and Islamic State destroyed us. How can we trust them anymore?

I put the defeats by Islamic State and criticism from the Yazidis to Major-General Selki.

He responded, 'First, let me say, our fighters fought bravely against Islamic State. We lost lots of valiant men on the battlefield.'

He declined to disclose or confirm the number of fatalities but I understood them to be in the low to mid hundreds. It could have been more.

He went on, 'Also, in war - and any soldier will tell you this - some battles you win, some you lose. But, to answer your question directly: you must remember the *pesh* had been defending a huge amount of territory. The battle front was 630 miles long. That's big for any military force.

Also, Islamic State took us by surprise. We never expected the attacks and when they came we didn't have enough weapons to defend ourselves. For every mortar round we fired, they fired a hundred back. We didn't know where wave after wave of jihadis were coming from. We lost contact with each other. It was chaos. I should also mention the Iraqi Army, supposedly our ally, simply melted away instead of coming to our rescue.'

I asked him, as a soldier, what was his judgement on the jihadists' fighting skills?

'Very well trained,' he said.

'We could recognise battlefield tactics they'd learned from Iraqi Army defectors, who, in turn, had been instructed by Western military trainers from countries like America.'

When the Kurdish Government called in US air strikes on August 8th and 9th 2014, the attackers were annihilated and the Kurds were able to launch a counter attack and recaptured Mosul Dam and nearby Kurdish towns.

American firepower enabled between 35,000 and 45,000 Yazidis trapped on Sinjar mountain to be evacuated to safety - although thousands still remain in refugee camps seven years later.

So what lessons had the *peshmerga* learned from the dark summer of 2014?

'We clearly needed better intelligence to anticipate when I.S. were going to strike,' said Major-General Selki

'We also should have been better armed. We also learned we must build trenches near our positions to stop Islamic State suicide bombers getting close to us in vehicles,' he added.

As I closed the interview, I asked his reaction to Islamic State leader Abu Bakir al-Baghdadi's death in a US special forces operation in October 2019, at a secret hideout on Syria's border with Turkey.

'As a leader, Al-Baghdadi was pretty much finished and ineffective anyway. 'His caliphate had been destroyed and it will never come back,' said the Major-General.

'What of former US President Donald Trump's repeated claims that Islamic State was "a hundred percent defeated"? He's wrong. Islamic State, as movement is not finished, just because Al-Baghdadi is dead.'

He added, 'Our intelligence is: there around 10,000 to 15,000 jihadi fighters still active, mostly in west Iraq, in Al Anbar and Ninevah provinces. The closest ones to us are in Makhmour, forty miles away, which isn't far.'

Major-General Selki closed our conversation with a chilling prediction, 'I believe in two to three years there will be a new jihadist movement. We've already seen evidence of new cells developing in Hadhar and Baradash in Ninevah province, in Hamden, near Kirkuk and in the Karamouch mountains. We've already observed them testing explosives and undergoing other training,' he warned.

He agreed the Islamic State movement was one of the most murderous and fanatical terror group the world had seen in modern times.

Major-General Selki continued, 'Let's be clear: what comes next in terms of jihadi activity will be even worse, Islamic State were ruthless and lacked humanity, but in general a lot of their attacks were on military targets. The next jihadist group will, I'm fairly certain, focus on civilians. I expect they've already formed sleeper cells, ready to strike.'

* On January 22 2021 Islamic State claimed responsibility for a twin suicide bombing – the deadliest in nearly three years - that ripped through a crowded market in central Baghdad, killing thirty-two people and injuring 110 others.

The first attacker drew a crowd at the bustling market in the capital's Tayaran Square by claiming to feel sick, then detonated his explosives belt.

As more people then flocked to the scene to help the victims, a second suicide bomber set off his explosives.

The open-air market, where second-hand clothes are sold at stalls, had been teeming with people after the lifting of nearly a year of COVID-19 restrictions.

*On January 29th, 2021 the U.S.-led military coalition killed a top Islamic State leader in Iraq in an airstrike intended to beat back a resurging terror campaign after the double suicide bombing in Baghdad the week before.

The coalition announced that Jabbar Salman Ali Farhan al-Issawi, forty-three, known as Abu Yasser, was killed in a joint mission with U.S. and Iraqi forces.

His 'death is another significant blow to Daesh resurgence efforts in Iraq,' said coalition spokesman Wayne Marotto, referring to the group by its Arabic acronym.

'The Coalition will continue to remove key leaders from the battlefield and degrade the terrorist organization. Terrorists - you will never live in peace - you will be pursued to the ends of the earth,' he added.

16. Dara

Before I dive into several chapters about the Kurds' unfulfilled quest for independence, I want to tell you about to my good friend Dara Yarra.

He's a man to whom I will always be indebted, for it was he who introduced me to a land called Kurdistan.

I first met him by pure happenstance when I worked as a reporter for the radio news service Independent Radio News (IRN), based in Gough Square, London in the mid-1980s.

Dara thought the world should know about the suffering of the Kurds under Saddam and he had IRN on his list because it pumped out news every hour to the UK's commercial radio stations; a big audience of around ten million.

At the time, Baghdad's genocidal campaign against the Kurds hadn't been on the mainstream news's agenda and, to be frank, like many Western journalists, I confess, I was unfamiliar with Iraqi Kurdistan, or exactly where it was on the map.

I was on a reporting shift one morning, on a busy news day, when the doorman at the Gough Square studios, Peter Thacker, ambled down to newsroom and yelled above the cacophony of clattering of typewriters: 'Oi news desk... there's a dodgy looking geezer upstairs. Claims he's Kurdish...from Iraq. Says he won't go away until he's spoken to a journo.'

'I told him to write in, but he still won't piss off!' shouted Peter above the din.

In Peter's defence I should say, media organisations like IRN were often approached with 'news tips' from people wandering in from the street, which, most times, proved to be of no interest.

My news editor, Vince McGarry, paused from bashing out the lead story and leaned over to me and said, 'John, go up and have a word'.

'He's been here before and he's a pest. See if he actually has a story. If not, tell him to fuck off and not come back!'

Of course, Dara did have a massive story to tell, a compelling one, about the Kurds' persecution by Saddam and I turned his interview into short news report for the network.

Dara and I have remained friends for thirty five years since that first newsroom encounter.

Like so many Kurdish politicians of a certain age, Dara personifies the remarkable, indomitable, Kurdish spirit.

As a young man Dara had been a *Peshmerga* commander fighting Saddam's forces in mountains close to Sulaimaniyah, in Iraqi Kurdistan's south east.

He was injured in a rocket attack, captured by Saddam's forces and, like thousands of his comrades, he was banished from the predominantly Sunni Kurdish region to live in mainly Shia districts of southern Iraq, including Basrah in the far south and Amarah, on the south eastern border with Iran.

As part of a plan to keep him on the move and nowhere long enough for him to cause trouble, the regime then forced him live in Al-Ramadi in Iraq's central west region. He was arrested again and tortured in Baghdad by the *mukhabarat*, or secret police.

Like other victims of the regime he's reluctant to talk about his physical suffering in jail, but the torturers' modus operandi included beating prisoners with copper wire, rubber hoses and wooden planks. The removal of prisoners' teeth and fingernails with pliers, was almost routine.

After years of torture Dara was eventually freed and, like thousands of dissident Iraqis, fled his homeland to arrive in the UK as a refugee, where he enrolled at Birmingham University and completed a master's degree.

Even in Europe he still wasn't safe. Like many dissidents who'd sought sanctuary in the west he soon discovered the long tentacles of the *mukhabarat* stretched across the world.

Using Iraqi missions in major cities in Europe and the US, Saddam's secret agents tracked down dissidents like Dara and, after carrying out an assassination, they'd ship the body back to Baghdad in a box marked *Diplomatic,* so no one in customs had the authority to examine or open it.

Dara very nearly became a victim of this kill policy.

He told me: 'I took a short holiday in southern Spain in the 1980s. I was walking down an ordinary street, minding my own business, when a large truck barrelled towards me. I could see it was trying to mow me down.

Somehow I managed to leap out of the way. Spanish police, who investigated the incident, told me they had intelligence it was an Iraqi hit squad. I was lucky I wasn't killed. It was definitely an assassination attempt.'

Dara was among Kurdish exiles who returned to Iraq after the toppling of Saddam Hussein in 2003, when he became an adviser to the newly formed Kurdish Regional Government.

He then became an Iraqi government minister; he's currently deputy minister at the Ministry of Construction, Housing, Municipalities and General Works and oversees a reconstruction fund for communities in Iraq affected by terrorism.

Dara maintains a home in West London and before I made my last research trip to Kurdistan, we met over dinner when we chatted about the Kurdish character and what made Kurds tick?

'John, we're patient people with white hearts, not black hearts, he said.

'That means, we're faithful friends. We trust and believe in the best in others. We expect the same in return. But, our trusting nature gets us into trouble. It makes us open to being easily betrayed.'

He is so right, as we shall see in the following chapters.

17. The long march

Independence: 'freedom from being governed by another country... the ability to live your life without being helped or influenced by other people.'
THE CAMBRIDGE DICTIONARY

It would be impossible to write a book about the Kurds without dedicating a substantial part of it to their struggle for independence. The next seven chapters are about that, so far, un-won battle.

The first green shoots of the Kurdish independence movement appeared at the end of the nineteenth century, when nomadic clan chiefs, stopped their wanderings and began staking claim to swathes of Mesopotamia's fertile soil.

After the First World War a serious attempt at independence was made when a delegation of Kurdish tribal leaders made the long journey to Paris to attend the 1919 Peace Conference where they tried to plead their case before America's President Woodrow Wilson, Britain's Prime Minister Lloyd George and the leaders of France, Italy and Japan.

It didn't go well. The Kurdish tribal chiefs reached the conference centre at the Versailles' spectacular Hall of Mirrors, but they were simply lost in the crush of dozens of other delegations like the Tongans.

Few at the Peace Conference knew who the Kurds were so no one took the men from Mesopotamia seriously. They returned home largely unheard and frustrated.

But just a year later, as part of the dismemberment of the Ottoman empire, Britain, France, Italy and Japan signed the Treaty of Sèvres which conditionally promised the Kurds the Holy Grail of independence.

The important clauses in the Treaty were: articles sixty-two and sixty-four.

Sixty-two defined the boundaries:

A Commission shall draft, a scheme of local autonomy for the Kurdish areas lying east of the Euphrates, south of the southern boundary of Armenia and north of the frontier of Turkey with Syria and Mesopotamia.

And article sixty-four contained a conditional promise:

If within one year the Kurdish peoples shall address themselves to the Council of the League of Nations to show that a majority of the population of these areas desires independence from Turkey, and if the Council considers these peoples are capable of independence and recommends that it should be granted to them, Turkey agrees to execute such a recommendation, and to renounce all rights and title over these areas.

So far, so good, you might say.

But crucially, British imperial interests in the region, including London's promise to the Arabs of their own state, were totally at odds with the concept of Kurdish independence.

The British controlled the Kurdish region under a mandate agreed in the Sykes-Picot Pact and to get an understanding of London's view of the 'southern Kurds,' I turned to records held by The National Archives at Kew in West London.

An archivist handed me a dossier compiled in 1919 written by Sir Mark Sykes - shortly before he fell victim to Spanish Flu and died at the Paris Peace Conference, mentioned earlier.

It was titled: 'The Kurdish Tribes of the Ottoman Empire,' and was based on Sykes's expeditions to the Kurdish region and reports by other British military officers: Captain C.F. Woolley and Major Edward Noel.

I should warn Kurdish friends that the dossier is couched in language used by imperial government officials a hundred years ago.

The tone will be offensive to twenty-first century ears and will be judged by many as a towering embodiment of arrogance by an imperial power.

But, here goes!

First, there's this candid description of the Kurdish people:

The natives are wild and ignorant and unwilling to give information about themselves to foreigners.

They live under the rule of tribal chiefs and are constantly at war with one another.

Very few are at all educated, for they have not the intelligence to grasp abstract ideas; their genius is practical rather than speculative.

Nomadic Kurdish tribal leaders in Turkey were characterised as:

Corrupt and degenerate intriguers.

They oppress their tenants, devour men's property and are always ready to go into partnership with a corrupt Turkish official to swindle the government.

Sir Mark's dossier was notably scathing about Kurdish communities, near the Turkish town of Erzurum:

They are a distinct and easily distinguishable race of tall, heavily built men, of surpassing ugliness of face and peculiar uncouthness of behaviour.

They are seemingly true nomads by instinct and lack any capacity for war or agriculture; they appear at once stupid and treacherous, disloyal, rapacious and quarrelsome; they must, however, have some qualities that are not apparent.

The dossier includes graphic descriptions of Kurdish inter tribal warfare and battles with the British military and Armenian Christians, who were struggling to maintain a toe hold in Mesopotamia.

Describing violence near Zarkho Sir Mark wrote:

At the end of March it was learnt the Kurds were massacring (sic) Christians in the district of Goyan, a short way north of Zakho, probably at the instigation of the Turks.

These acts of turbulence culminated on the 4th of April in the murder of Captain Pearson, a British political officer; he had gone to this district to investigate the massacres and to set up a force of gendarmerie, when he was attacked and killed by Goyan Kurds.

The murderers cut off their victim's ears and sent them to Abd-ur-Rahman, Agha of the Shernakhli Kurds, who sent back presents in return. All the tribes were greatly excited by the news of the murder.

Sir Mark's report does include kinder passages about the Kurdish people:

Kurds are usually good agriculturalists; many semi-nomads are weavers and smiths by trade. They treat their women (who are not veiled) kindly; they are generous and very hospitable.

In battle they are courageous and much more cool than the Arabs; they are callous in shedding human blood and generally very brutal. In war they are often treacherous, but simple in ordinary life.

At a more banal level we learn from Sir Mark's report that Kurdish was used as an everyday language, but it had no written form, so letters and legal and official documents had to be written in Arabic or Turkish.

Kurdish towns and villages are described in great detail and I enjoyed this colourful dispatch about a community near Lake Van in Turkey:

The men wear the most extraordinary clothes, buttons of pearls, collars, and cuffs of black velvet, baggy trousers and sashes; the richer tribesmen also wear a collar and tie; on the head they wear an enormous tarbush of white felt, about a foot high and bulging out like a busby, round which a very small turban of silk is wound.

Another peculiarity is that they wear long hair and careful-ly-trimmed whiskers on each side of the face. The women as well as the men shave the top of the head.

The report has detail about how Kurdish communities generated income:

The climate is rather hot in summer, for the town faces the south; in winter, snow accumulates to a great depth; on the whole, it is a healthy place, though rheumatism is said to be common.

There are chalybeate and sulphur-springs in the neighbour-hood. Water is abundant; small springs also are numerous. The main exports are grain, fleeces, wools, hides, skins, furs, gall-nuts, and gum-tragacanth. Coarse red cloth is manufactured in the town.

As an interesting side bar I also gleaned from Sir Mark's dossier that in 1919 the British Government knew there was oil under Kurdish soil, but there's no indication of any excitement about its potential. The reports says blandly:

About one and a half hours' journey to the east of Zakho are two areas of petroleum-springs, on the right bank of the Khabur.

Part of this petroleum (sic) is purified by the local Kurds in a cauldron-installation near the springs, but the larger part of the supply is sent for preparation to Zakho, where there are two cauldron-installations.

The residue consists of the by-products of tar, which serves for fuel to heat the cauldrons.

So why apparent British indifference about Kurdistan's oil potential?

Most of the world's oil came from Mexico or the United States in those days, and whatever reserves of 'black gold' lay beneath the surface in Kurdistan was unproven. And as any hydrocarbons expert will tell you: the discovery of traces of oil is no guarantee of vast wells.

As I read on I was curious whether the Sykes dossier revealed insight into the nascent Kurdish independence movement or evidence of a single Kurdish leader for Kurds to rally around? An independent nation needs a leader. Sir Mark gave this assessment:

The highly tribal Kurds seemed to be in disarray.
In regard to the question of Kurdish independence, the principle is regarded with favour by the leading men of the tribe, but no particular scheme seems to have been thought out.

Then, there was this contribution:

Major Noel quotes the following popular verse, well-known in Kurdistan, as reflecting the feelings of the average Kurdish peasant on the question of independence: 'If we had a King, He would be worthy of a crown; He should have a capital; And we should share his fortune; Turk and Persian and Arab; Would all be our slaves; But what can we do? Our market is dull: We have the goods but cannot find a buyer.'

Finally, Sykes considered whether the Kurds deserved their own independent nation. It seems: yes, but with a big caveat. It concluded:

Who can doubt that it is in the highest interests of the Kurds that they should be for ever liberated from Turkish misrule?

But to give them complete autonomy would be, in the words of a Greek poet, 'a gift that is no gift, but profitless'.

A half-savage race must pass many years in tutelage before it can learn truly to use and appreciate its liberty and to exercise self-government.

So it is with the Kurds; they cannot master at once the arts of civilisation, nor learn the maintenance of law and order, which it has taken the western nations of Europe nearly twenty centuries to evolve and to develop.

One of the Great Powers must accept a mandate to administer their country and must instil (sic) into the hearts of its people the lessons which other nations have learnt by their experience of centuries.

To summarise: although Sir Mark Sykes, and colleagues Captain C.F. Woolley and Major Edward Noel considered the Kurds had admirable cultural qualities, the overall conclusion in London was the Kurds were a bunch of fractious, uncultured peasants, who fought a lot amongst themselves, had no natural single leader, and only after a period of domination by a great power like Britain, could they be ready for independence.

18. 'The Kurd requires a beating.'

The Kurd has the mind of a schoolboy,
but without the schoolboy's innate cruelty.
He requires a beating one day and a sugar plum the next.
Too much spoiling or too much severity renders
him unmanageable... like a schoolboy
he will always lie to save himself.
MEMORANDUM TO LONDON FROM MAJOR W. R. HAY,
BRITISH GOVERNMENT OFFICIAL, ALEPPO, 1921

Winston Churchill was Britain's Secretary of State for the Colonies when Arab and Kurdish rebellions against British control boiled. Churchill's disdain was clear in this description of the region as:

A score of mud villages sandwiched in between a swampy river and a blistering desert, inhabited by a half-naked families, usually starving.

It was from this imperialist point of view the government in London set about crushing rebellions which were costing dear in British blood and treasure.

The Arab revolt of 1920, was arguably the most significant rebellion which began with mass protests in Baghdad, including demonstrations by embittered officers of the old Ottoman

Army, which quickly sparked secondary rebellions in the south including the Shia strongholds of Najaf and Karbala.

Those uprisings were put down by the British within months, but at a cost of at least 5,000 Iraqi lives; British and Indian regiments lost around 1,000 men.

Churchill was a great supporter of the fledgling Royal Air Force and he figured bombing from the air was the best method to bring the rebellious Mesopotamians to heel.

An air campaign was attractive because it meant a dramatic reduction in British casualties and was more cost effective than keeping tens of thousands of British soldiers on the ground, along with their military hardware, horses and supplies.

He also wanted to use the infantry in Mesopotamia to maintain security in India. And so in 1920 and 1921 RAF bomber pilots flew approximately 4000 hours and dropped a hundred tons of bombs on Arab and Kurdish communities.

Thousands on the ground died.

The British lost nine servicemen killed and eleven aircraft destroyed.

The Arab and Kurd now know what real bombing means... within forty-five minutes a full-sized village can be practically wiped out, and a third of its inhabitants killed or injured, by four or five machines which offer them no real target, no opportunity for glory as warriors, no effective means of escape,

reported RAF Squadron Leader, Arthur 'Bomber' Harris, who went on to perfect carpet bombing of German cities in World War Two.

Harris had also sanctioned use of delayed action bombs on rebellious villages, even though the weapons were outlawed under the 1907 Hague Convention.

Historians can't agree whether chemical weapons like chlorine or mustard gas were ever used by the British to quell Arab and Kurd uprisings, although we know Churchill was in favour of their use - he'd wanted to gas the Turks at Gallipoli in 1915 and as Minister for Munitions he ensured a third of shells fired by British guns contained mustard gas.

Seven decades before Saddam Hussein sparked world outrage for dropping gas shells on the Kurds, Churchill penned this War Office memorandum:

I don't understand the squeamishness about the use of gas.
I am strongly in favour of using poisoned gas against uncivilised tribes.

Although, he also added this line: *The loss of life should be reduced to a minimum.*

In a letter to Chief of Air Staff, Sir Hugh Trenchard, Churchill also wrote:

I think you should certainly proceed with the experimental work on gas bombs. Especially mustard gas, which would inflict punishment on recalcitrant natives without inflicting grave injury.

Although there's no clear evidence chemical weapons like mustard gas were used on *'recalcitrant natives'* in Iraq - had they been, it would have been considered a war crime today.

19. The Cairo Conference

In early 1921 the Middle East was still a mess.

The cost to the British Government of policing rebellious Mesopotamia was running at £2 billion a year - at today's values – and other troublesome matters had piled up in Secretary of State Winston Churchill's in-tray.

There was not only the Kurdish independence question to resolve but also the pledge by Britain to millions of Arabs of an independent state stretching from Palestine to Persia and the British undertaking to support a Jewish state in Palestine under the Balfour Agreement.

Churchill called a conference in the Egyptian capital, Cairo, in March 1921, in a bid to bring some order to the chaos.

Although his initiative seems to have been well meant he was pilloried in the British press for his efforts; his critics dubbed the conference a: *'durbar,'* and a 'magnificent gathering of the imperial court and its king'.

An amusing image indeed; and the Cairo Conference, as it turned out, did provide a couple of comedic moments.

As Churchill arrived at the conference venue, Cairo's palatial Semiramis Hotel, he was confronted by a mob of chanting Egyptian nationalists.

The ever jovial-but-truculent, Churchill who was a keen amateur artist and noted *bon viveur,* the same man who took Fortnum and Mason hampers with him to war, swept past demonstrators and into the hotel clutching a painting easel, followed by a valet gingerly carrying a bottle of wine in an ice-bucket.

What the protestors made of it isn't recorded.

Another amusing scene occurred when Churchill took time off from parleying round the conference table to paint the Great Pyramids at Giza.

He climbed aboard a camel to travel between locations at Giza, but managed to fall off the beast's hump, whereupon his worried guide and translator offered him a horse instead.

Churchill demurred and with typical grit, said: 'I've started on a camel, and I will finish on a camel.'

By the time the Cairo Conference opened civil servants in London's corridors of power had already drawn up a plan carve a new country out of Mesopotamia called Iraq - a name taken from the Sumerian word for the region: Urak.

London had also decided Iraq should be ruled by a puppet king loyal to Britain, a Hashemite royal in exile: King Faisal.

By creating a new country called Iraq this would fulfil Britain's promise of an independent state for the Arabs.

Meanwhile, British military spending would be cut because the main burden of keeping the peace could be handed to local chieftains.

The question of independence for the Kurds was still on the table for discussion at Cairo, but as the great and the good gathered in the Semiramis Hotel, Kurdish autonomy was already looking unlikely as the Kurds were about to be swallowed into a new country called Iraq ruled from Baghdad.

Imperial considerations had to come first and last.

Cairo Conference 1921.
(Gertude Bell second row, second left)

The Citadel, Erbil

20. Gertrude Bell

Churchill gathered a stellar cast of Middle East experts for the Cairo Conference, including Colonel T. E Lawrence – 'Lawrence of Arabia' Britain's High Commissioner in Baghdad, Sir Percy Cox, and Gertrude Bell.

Churchill jokingly called them his 'forty thieves'.

I digress to talk about Bell who was to play a key role in the future of the Kurds in Iraq and was, by any standards, a remarkable woman - as non-stereotypical Victorian female as you can get. Men among her contemporaries were in awe and disparaging of her, in equal measure.

The traveller and diplomat Sir Mark Sykes used less than diplomatic language to describe Bell as a: 'silly chattering windbag of conceited, gushing, flat-chested, man-woman, globe-trotting, rump-wagging, blethering ass!'

By contrast, Sir Percy Cox, a Colonial Office Minister in Baghdad paid her a backhanded compliment with words judged sexist today, 'She is a remarkably clever woman... with the brains of a man'.

On the other hand, Bell's reputation as an Arabist prompted Lord Cromer, a former British High Commissioner in Egypt to say, 'Miss Gertrude Bell knows more about the Arabs and Arabia than almost any other living English man or woman'.

Colonel Lawrence, might have disagreed with that.

Bell was born in 1868 to upper class parents in County Durham, in the north of England; her grandfather had been an industrialist and Member of the British Parliament.

Bell's mother died when she was three, giving birth to her brother.

She went on to have a lifelong close relationship with her father Sir Hugh Bell, a mill owner with a reputation for caring for his workers.

She read history at Oxford and before World War One had not only travelled alone across most of Europe, where she scaled the Swiss Alps including Mont Blanc, but had also journeyed extensively in the Middle East, which was remarkable for a female of that era.

Bell never married or had children. Her only true beau: Lieutenant Colonel Charles Doughty-Wylie, was tragically killed at the Battle of Gallipoli in April 1915.

She spoke six languages, including Arabic and Persian and published several books about her travels across what the Romans called *Arabia Deserta*.

Bell was hired by Britain's Secret Service in 1915 for her map-making abilities and her knowledge of the Middle East.

In the film version of *The English Patient*, British soldiers ask: 'How do we get through mountains?' and one says: 'The Bell map shows the way'.

Whilst usually based in Cairo she also kept homes in Baghdad and Basrah, living the life of an English *memsahib*; a gilded world of servants, duck shoots, pony rides and swimming parties.

If you're ever in Basrah you can still see what's left of one of Bell's homes on the banks of the Shatt Al-Arab canal.

When I was last in the city I was surprised the wood-framed, mansion was still standing, more or less, given its front line position during the Iran Iraq war in the 1980s, when so many bloody battles were waged in streets nearby and other houses had been blown to smithereens.

Falling masonry and rotting wooden support beams didn't seem to worry impoverished families from the Iraqi Marshes who'd moved in as squatters in Bell's former home.

I reckon Bell, who cherished Iraq and the Iraqis, would have had no objection to its new occupants.

Luckily for us, many of Bell's chatty, and sometimes indiscreet, letters home to her father Sir Hugh and her stepmother Florence Bell in England, have survived and give a fascinating insight, not only into Bell's colourful life, but also illuminating detail about what she and London government officials thought about Kurdish independence.

In 1918, Bell wrote home to her stepmother: *I've rather lost my heart to the Kurds.*

And January 22nd 1921, two months before Cairo, she wrote to her father:

Some sort of local Kurdish government we must have, preferably connected with Mesopotamia, for the advantage of all concerned; the only alternative is to move out and leave it to chaos.

I get from that she didn't favour total Kurdish autonomy and in a paper Churchill asked her to write in 1919 it seems she thought the warring Kurds weren't ready for independence. Bell wrote:

The occupants of northern Mesopotamia (namely the Kurds) since prehistory, were constantly at war with their neighbours, the entire area is a mix of many races and creeds: Sunni, Shia and Christian.

Bell mentioned Kurdish tribal chiefs calling for independence, but wrote:

What they mean by that neither they nor anyone else knows... so much for Kurdish nationalism!

21. The Kurdish question

In an effort to find out what happened at the Cairo Conference and how the 'Kurdish question' was handled I delved further into The National Archives in Kew, West London where an assistant handed me a bundle of faded, tissue-thin documents, bound with pink ribbon.

Although the front cover was stamped *'Secret,'* the dossier had been declassified and was made public in 1972.

From this file I learned promises to the Kurds under the Treaty of Sèvres about independence were debated at Cairo Conference on the morning of March 15th 1921.

Churchill was in the chair. There were seven others present: Britain's High Commissioner in Baghdad, Sir Percy Cox, Gertrude Bell, Colonel T. E. Lawrence, Major Edward Noel, a British political officer from Sulaimaniyah, and Major H. W. Young. Major R. D. Badock took notes.

Paging through the flimsy papers I learned there was an acknowledgement that the Kurds had been promised autonomy however that proposal sit well with London's plans for a new country called Iraq ruled by an Arab king which included, for economic reasons, fertile and oil rich Kurdish territory near Mosul and Kirkuk.

Churchill asked Colonel Lawrence for his opinion. Lawrence was adamant the Kurds would never accept rule from Baghdad by an Arab king, the implication being Lawrence thought the Kurds should be allowed to run their own autonomous region themselves.

Bell suggested fudging the issue. She proposed pushing the question of Kurdish independence to the back burner for six months, by which time Faisal would be enthroned, and according to Bell: the Kurds would accept his rule - once they'd got used to the idea.

The minutes showed Churchill reminded the meeting Kurdish autonomy shouldn't be overlooked and made it clear he backed a proposal from Major Young.

His suggestion was to include the Kurds in a new country called Iraq, but under the oversight of the British High Commissioner in Baghdad Sir Percy Cox, in the same way the British Governor General of South Africa administered Rhodesia at the time.

Churchill went on to indicate his support for a separate Kurdish army, under the command of British officers, to relieve British troops in Mosul and Kirkuk in October that year.

And that seems to have been it. The fate of the so-called 'southern Kurds' had been sealed.

Gertrude Bell was detailed to draw the map of the new Iraq merging the former Ottoman provinces of Basrah in the south, the central region of Baghdad and also Mosul in the north - the latter including the Kurdish areas up to the Persian border.

As the Cairo conference wound down Churchill telegraphed his Prime Minister, David Lloyd George tell him 'mission accomplished,' and he and his 'forty thieves' moved on to Jerusalem.

You can see why Churchill was satisfied.

The pledge of a separate country for the Arabs ruled by an Arab king had been honoured, Britain's military budget for the region would be slashed, British interests on the ground would be protected on the cheap by local armies under British control and the religious makeup of Iraq would be maintained by incorporating the Sunni Kurds to balance against the predominantly Shia south.

Everyone was happy, except, of course, the Kurds who'd suffered what is still seen by them today as the first of a series of double-dealings and betrayals by Western powers.

And a gloomy Colonel Lawrence, who was firmly against the new arrangement for the Kurds, said of Churchill's *durbar*: 'It has been one of the longest fortnights I have ever lived.'

*The mahogany table, on which Bell sketched her historic map, which memorialised the Kurds' inclusion in Iraq, had pride of place in the dining room of the British Embassy in Baghdad when I visited in 2013. The then Ambassador, Michael Aaron, showed it to me, with some pleasure.

22. The King of Kurdistan

Perhaps predictably, the best-laid plans made at Cairo soon fell apart in the early 1920s.

Turkish militias made repeated raids into northern Iraq where they won ground and bought off Kurdish tribal chiefs with cash rewards for loyalty. By pumping money in the Turks established a vice-like grip through institutionalised corruption.

In a further effort to undermine British overall control, the Turks fostered enmity between Kurdish tribal chiefs prompting Kurd on Kurd skirmishes in a classic divide and rule strategy. Bell wrote about this to her father, from Baghdad in July 1922:

We hope the idiotic Kurdish tribes on the frontier will be discouraged from throwing in their lot with the 300 or so Turks

She followed up with this on August 18th 1922:

Affairs on the Kurdistan frontier are also a great anxiety. The Kemalists (Turks) are definitely coming down into Sulaymaniyah, not in great force, but raising the tribes with Islamic propaganda.

And we have nothing but a small levy column, exhausted by two months hard marching in the heat, and aeroplanes which aren't very effective in that mountain country.

I feel terribly anxious about our isolated officers and scarcely less about one or two of the big Kurdish Aghas (tribal leaders) who are standing by us so manfully.

No doubt spurred on by Turkey's destabilisation efforts, Kurdish tribal leaders relaunched their push for independence with vigour.

One chieftain stood out from the rest. He was Sheikh Mahmud Barzanji who stunned the British by boldly declaring himself: King of Kurdistan.

At first, London tolerated the popular, moustachioed leader because he was a man who could bring peace to the rebellious south east including the major city of Sulaimaniyah.

Of Sheikh Barzanji, Bell wrote, on August 15th 1922:

Sheikh Mahmud is just the ordinary type of Kurdish robber baron, only a little more so. He has no idea of administration,

He will job all his friends and relations into office and oppress, not to say murder, his enemies.

We can't stop him, nor yet could any Englishman assume responsibility for what he'll do.

But if we keep on good terms with him and uphold as far as we can the independence of that bit of Kurdistan which is under him.

But London's tolerance of Barzanji didn't have the desired effect because he continued launching revolts against British occupation.

Here's Bell's account of the battle for control of Sulaimaniyah and the loss of British soldiers' lives including a decorated officer Captain Robert Makant. The Kurdish 'agha' she refers to is Barzanji. Bell wrote to her father on June 22nd 1922:

We've had another disaster - lost two most gallant officers owing to the treachery of a Kurdish agha (tribal chief) who attempted to murder a Kurdish official, and turned, snapping like a dog, on the two Englishmen who came to adjust terms with him.

One of them, the Levy officer, Capt. Makant, I knew very well and loved.

He was a most enchanting creature, straight and brave and absorbed in his job. I rode his black horse all along the Persian frontier last year.

What fine lives we have wasted there - well, I won't say wasted yet, but it's a heavy price we're paying for the redemption of that lawless land.

The murder of Captain Makant and another British officer, Captain Bond, was debated in the British House of Commons where Churchill was already taking criticism about the continued loss of British military lives in the Kurdish region. On June 27th 1922 Churchill thundered:

Troops are moving; both cavalry and infantry are operating in the district, the Air Force is reconnoitring (sic) in the air, and we hope to bring the authors of this disgustingly treacherous breach of a parley to which these officers had been bidden to summary punishment and execution in the shortest possible time.

The British decided they'd had enough of the King of Kurdistan and he had to go.

We have this deliciously amusing description of one failed assassination attempt in one of Bell's letters in December 1923:

Accordingly on Xmas Day, the Air Marshal himself sallied forth with the utmost secrecy; he flew over Sulaimaniyah 150 ft from the ground, spotted Sheikh Mahmud's house, dropped countless bombs on it and flew back congratulating himself on having made an end of the rogue.

Next day came a telegram from Sheikh Mahmud saying that he was in the best of health and couldn't understand why we had bombed Sulaimaniyah, that's all we know at present.

Barzanji was eventually captured by British forces, tried and sentenced to death. The death penalty was commuted to a prison term and he was packed off to serve his time in a British fort in India.

But, during his absence, Kurdish rebellions erupted again and the British were forced to bring him back to calm things down.

Barzanji, the man who would be King of Kurdistan, survived further assassination attempts and from 1942 he lived in relative obscurity in a village near Sulaimaniyah, until his death in 1956, aged 79.

Barzanji outlived Gertrude Bell by thirty years and today remains an inspiration for the Kurdish independence movement.

Bell, on the other hand, was sidelined from her role in the administration of Iraq and suffered a sad end.

She died, aged just 57, on July 12th 1926 in her Baghdad home, short of money and, by her own admission: lonely.

She'd taken sleeping tablets the night before and there was speculation she'd taken her own life, although suicide was never proved.

A British doctor at the Royal Hospital, Baghdad, gave Bell's cause of death simply as: barbiturate poisoning.

No suicide note was found, although she'd asked a colleague the day before to take care of her dog, 'if anything happened to her'.

The Iraqi government Bell helped bring to power was overthrown in 1958. A series of military coups and deepening repression followed under Saddam Hussein.

The National Museum Bell founded in 1926 was looted in the aftermath of the US led invasion in 2003 and although renovated, thousands of its artefacts are still missing.

At the time of writing the regime in Baghdad, led by Prime Minister Mustafa Al-Kadhimi is effectively bankrupt and as corrupt as ever. Iranian backed Shia militias seem to be out of the government's control, dangerous tensions have grown between Erbil and Baghdad and for the long suffering Iraqis most have no access to a clean water supply or national electricity grid.

Kurdish chief c1900

Qazi Mohammed, President of first Kurdish republic

23. The Cairo legacy

As we've heard, Bell's map of a new country known as Iraq sealed things in a very bad way for the nation's Kurdish population.

With a stroke of her cartographer's pen, people known as Southern Kurds had been swallowed up into an Arab ruled nation with powerful neighbours at every turn, including Persia and Turkey.

As for Turkey's Kurds: the final blow for their independence hopes was delivered in the Treaty of Lausanne in 1923, which superseded the Treaty of Sèvres.

British Foreign Secretary, Lord Curzon made all the right noises and championed the Kurdish cause for autonomy, telling delegates, 'the Kurds with their independent history, customs, manners and character ought to be an autonomous race'.

But, Mustafa Kemal Ataturk, the victorious and towering leader of Turkey's war of independence, said he could never compromise on Turkish sovereignty and when it came to the treaty's fine print the British government dropped Curzon's demand - indeed, the treaty didn't mention the Kurds at all and resulted in fifty per cent of the Kurdish population being included in the newly defined borders of Turkey.

With echoes of what Iraqi Kurds branded a British betrayal at the Cairo Conference, London had once again cut a shabby deal with Ankara and had been party to extinguishing independence hopes for Turkey's Kurds also.

Curzon said afterwards, 'I do not feel very confident, but I hope for the best.' He was wrong to be optimistic.

As the century progressed the Kurds didn't exist in the eye of the Turkish state. Kurdish names were replaced with Turkish names, the Kurdish language was banned. Kurds were forcefully assimilated into being Turkish. Large Kurdish populations in Turkey fled to neighbouring Syria during violent Turkification campaigns in the first half of the 20th century.

More than 40,000 died in the conflict between Kurdish insurgent groups and the Turkish state. Executions of civilians, forced displacements, destroyed villages, arbitrary arrests and disappearances of Kurdish journalists, activists and politicians filled that dark decade of the 1990s.

Turkey's Kurds enjoyed relative peace between 2005 and 2015 when the Justice and Development Party government partly lifted restrictions on Kurdish language, allowed Kurdish media and started a peace process. In the June 2015 general election, the Peoples' Democratic Party, or the H.D.P., the pro-Kurdish party, crossed a ten per cent threshold required to enter Parliament and won eighty seats.

Unfortunately, the shaky peace process fell apart and the conflict between the Turkish forces and the Kurdish insurgents resumed and continues to this day.

I conclude this chapter by addressing the charge that the decision taken in Cairo by Churchill and his 'forty thieves' to include the Kurdish region in Iraq led to decades of bloodshed and untold misery for the Kurds, who are still paying the price today.

With the benefit of twenty-first century hindsight, the claim is absolutely correct. No one can disagree.

However, can I step in here and be counsel for the defence for Churchill and his cohorts? Consider what was happening on the ground in Mesopotamia in 1921 when the fateful decision was made.

According to reliable records noted in earlier chapters of this book: at the time of the Cairo Conference there was no sense of Kurdish unity of purpose and whilst tribalism is arguably one of the Kurds' greatest strengths, in that people within the clan feel safe, it's also their Achilles heel.

Clan rivalries meant princely Kurdish fiefdoms were constantly fighting each other and as we heard from Gertrude Bell and British government officials: Sir Mark Sykes, Captain C.F. Woolley and Major Edward Noel, inter-tribal warfare was a major stumbling in block in Kurdish claims for independence.

Even today, a hundred years later, there's recurring, intense rivalry, between the two main political blocs in Iraqi Kurdistan.

But what if the Kurds had stopped fighting each other and had been united in 1921 under their own strong Kurdish leader - what then?

Full autonomy for land-locked Kurdistan still wouldn't have worked as the Kurds didn't have a basic government infrastructure in place or have sufficient natural resources to function economically as a separate nation in a post-World War One world. As we heard, life was so basic the Kurdish language didn't even have a written form.

Under the Cairo plan to include the Kurdish region in a new country called Iraq meant the fledgling nation would have a functioning central government in Baghdad and boundaries that embraced the fertile Kurdish plains surrounding Mosul and the oil fields of Kurdish Kirkuk; riches to share with the whole country, including the Kurds.

There were other compelling reasons why it was the correct decision to include the Kurdish region.

In 1921 the Turks were intent on destabilising Iraq's northern border region as part of a plan to seize control of Kurdish territory from the British. It made sense therefore to create a Kurdish a buffer zone against Turkish incursions.

Meanwhile, King Faisal had raised his real fears that if the Kurds were granted independence they might align themselves with neighbouring Persia and turn on Baghdad.

For all those reasons - members of the jury - I would argue Churchill and his colleagues made the right decision in 1921 to include the Kurdish region in Iraq - at that time.

After the Cairo Conference there was a golden era when oil revenues flowed and Iraq including the Kurdish region was relatively stable.

Then came catastrophe. In 1958 there was a military coup and the entire Iraqi royal family including King Faisal II were machine-gunned to death in a palace courtyard.

Ultimately the Baathists gained power and there has been no stability and unity in Iraq since.

Countless hundreds of thousands of military and innocent civilians have died, especially during the rule of Saddam Hussein, and even today young Iraqis are being shot in the streets in long running protests against one corrupt Baghdad regime after another.

Hindsight is, of course, a wonderful thing and I can't deny the British decision in 1921 to carve a new country out of Mesopotamia called Iraq, turned out to be a disastrous, not only for the Kurds, but all Iraqis.

It's sometimes called: 'Churchill's Folly'.

Had she been alive I think Gertrude Bell would, with huge regret, have agreed. Writing to her father years after the Cairo Conference her words had a brutal honesty:

We rushed into the business with our usual disregard for a comprehensive political scheme.

Muddle through! Why yes, we do, wading through blood and tears that need never have been shed.

24. Driving with Mustafa

Once upon a time... there were railway lines and one or two trains... during the last century... in the age of steam.

Ottoman and British engineers built stations and rail tracks at Erbil, Kirkuk and Mosul in the early 1900s, and the Iraqi Oil Company laid down a line between Kirkuk and Erbil in 1947.

Mosul was a station on the foolishly ambitious Berlin to Baghdad railway, a folly which took forty years to build before World War Two intervened and the project hit the buffers.

Through decades of war and peace Kurdistan's railway stations have fallen apart and the lines rusted away or sold for scrap.

I did hear whispers the Chinese wanted to build a high-speed rail-link between Erbil and Sulaimaniyah, but like a lot more big projects talked up in Kurdistan, it hasn't materialised so far.

So, with no trains, if you want to travel anywhere in northern Iraq, it has to be by road.

I've never mustered enough courage to actually get behind the wheel of a car in Kurdistan. I used to have a regular 'chauffeur'.

Mustafa was wiry, smiley, married and in his early thirties with a penchant for 1950s leather motorcycle jackets.

For his one-man taxi driving business he drove a battered off-white Mercedes with a rear bumper tied on with a bit of wire.

Although punctuality wasn't his strong suit Mustafa was otherwise very reliable and jovially good company.

Crucially, he had the good sense to know when to put his foot down when journalistic deadlines loomed.

At the start of any assignment Mustafa launched into fast moving traffic without looking.

There was lots of screeching tyres, horns blaring and cussing from other motorists, but it was all more to follow form, rather than genuine road rage. Everybody did it.

Mustafa drove with his window wound down in all weathers.

That was to accommodate an outstretched arm and pinched fingers, to indicate a late lane change, or more often to show disgust at another driver's lack of road skills – once we'd safely overtaken them.

Morning appointments meant an early start and Mustafa would often pull over sharply at a roadside cafe *en route* with the precision of a knife thrower and shout, 'Breakfast, Mr John?'

I didn't ever make a fuss about an early meal-break, because a Kurdish breakfast is one of the world's best: a lump of goat cheese, a hard-boiled egg, naan bread, pillows of creamy yoghourt, generous dollops of golden honey and a steaming cup of *chai* (tea) in a fluted glass, with at least three teaspoons of sugar.

My favourite part was swirling the warm flat-bread in the honey and yoghurt. Delicious!

It makes my mouth water even writing about it.

Although being hired by me to drive from A to B it was gregarious Mustafa's practice to pick up a random of cast of his pals to join us on journeys.

We'd stop suddenly on a street corner and a man would hop in the back.

'This my friend, Mr John, he's coming with us.'

'Fine,' I'd say, hesitantly... 'why not?'

Other characters would also make an appearance like: Mustafa's mother.

Once, driving in Erbil I'd noted we were heading east, instead of north to my destination.

'Mr John,' said Mustafa in a cold serious tone.

'My mother sick. I promised I'd take her to the doctor this morning.'

Only the heartless would have said: 'screw, your mother, I'm paying you to take me to an interview and we're late, let's get going.'

So mother was collected and after a lot of *salaams* and kissy-kissy from dutiful son, mum joined us in the back for a trip to a clinic.

There was an odd innocence to it all, so it was hard to be angry.

The actual mechanics of driving: using foot pedals, the steering wheel and indicators, was never really enough for Mustafa.

Even a shouty conversation with me or a random travelling companion in the rear seat didn't fill the mental void which, it seemed, could only be filled with music and making and receiving calls on one of three mobile phones.

Music was as essential to the journey as a full tank of gas and meant fiddling with Bluetooth, the radio and CDs with both hands whilst driving.

I noticed he was very adept at looking for a music source while controlling the steering wheel with both knees.

Music was always played at maximum volume and the lyrics of Kurdish hits tend to be upbeat and jolly.

A translation would be along the lines of: my girlfriend's madly in love with me, my best pal is home on leave from *peshmerga* duties, so let's party!

On the other hand, the Arab version would be melancholy: my girlfriend's left me and my best friend's gone in the army so I'm sitting sad at home.

On the open highway the legal top speed was an optional sixty-two miles per hour. That meant foot down time, nudging ninety at least, especially on the highway from Erbil to Sulaimaniyah through stretches of mountainous wilderness.

In a land with no rigid observance of driving laws, I always found it curious that like most Kurdish drivers, Mustafa avoided overtaking on the inside.

This rule was followed even when there was a fellow in a Land Cruiser stubbornly blocking the outer lane.

Mustafa would inch up to Mr Land Cruiser's back bumper, flash his headlights and sound the taxi's horn.

Land Cruiser would ignore him, at first.

It would take prolonged obligatos on the horn and more headlight flashing until Mr Land Cruiser would swerve into the slow lane in a dramatic manner as if the idea had occurred to him impulsively and by some serendipitous inspiration.

Apart from the eccentric behaviour of Kurdish drivers in general, I recall three other major road hazards on Kurdish highways.

Number one peril: speed humps on a broad, straight highway - they're rarely signposted. But Kurdish drivers don't need signposts, they have a sixth sense about these things; like a horse's ability to smell fear. Even if they haven't driven the road before they always manage to drop speed in time and roll over the bump in the highway effortlessly. It's uncanny.

The second danger: overtaking on blind corners.

Many a time in oil-rich Kurdistan, as Mustafa pulled out to overtake, a fully-laden fuel tanker would loom from the opposite direction. With both traveling at speed, that scenario could end in a horrible conflagration between taxi and truck. Not in Kurdistan. Mustafa would see the behemoth heading towards us, but he still overtook at speed; I'd clutch my seat in a sweat and held my breath.

Mustafa's Kurdish sixth sense of spacial awareness served us well and we always - yes, always - missed tankers with just inches to spare.

The third hazard in Kurdistan is when you spot an eruption of red tail-lights and clouds of billowing white dust in the far distance.

It means the tarmac road has run out and morphed into a dirt track because the government has run out of cash - again. Mustafa would hit the brakes, switch on hazard warning lights and, in a scene of agitated anarchy at the point where tarmac turns to dust, he'd bunch up with truckers, other cars and motorcycles to squeeze onto the single-lane dirt-road, with no problem.

Mile after mile there's a sense of eternality on dead straight Kurdish roads.

In summer, when the heat leaps out like a hammer and temperatures are north of forty centigrade, it's fascinating to watch cars and trucks on the long road ahead being swallowed into glistening mirage and then vanish; oncoming vehicles materialise out of the horizon's incandescence like ghosts.

The golden rule about driving in Kurdistan is stay on your toes and expect the unexpected.

Sometimes cars and trucks coming in the opposite direction cross the central reservation and come at you on your hard shoulder.

No worries: it's what they do.

The safe arrival at a destination with Mustafa was always a triumph of heartfelt sighs and broad grins, because as everyone knows: all journeys in Kurdistan are completed safely when God wills it.

One stand out road incident for me and my cameraman in the land of the Kurds was in Turkey on a long highway from the Iranian border to the Turkish city of Diyarbakir. Traffic was scarce, partly because we were in a war zone and sensible, normal folk were stayed indoors.

We rattled westwards, scratchy loudspeakers on taxi driver Mehmet's CD player sand-blasted our ears, but the unmistakable smell of roast beef wafted in through the open car windows.

As the miles slipped by, the aroma grew stronger, to the extent our mouths began to water. I was even beginning to visualise gravy and Yorkshire puddings.

But where the heck was the roast beef smell coming from?

Mehmet assured us he hadn't left a chunk of steak on the engine block under the bonnet, so there was absolutely no logical explanation for the delicious aroma. That was, until we breezed over the brow of a hill.

Ahead of us was a moving lorry pulling a dead cow on a rope. The road's friction was cooking the deceased beast as the truck trundled along.

In that part of the world, trucks occasionally drive to market with a cow tethered and trotting behind and Mehmet ventured the cow had been alive at the start of its last journey but at some point gave up the ghost.

As we overtook the truck and dead cow Mehmet had a shouted conversation with the driver.

The lorry driver apparently knew the cow had died *en route* but he was heading to a slaughter house anyway. So that's alright then!

25. Remembering Anfal

You can go online for masses of historical and erudite detail about Saddam Hussein's *Anfal* campaign against the Kurds.

Anfal means spoils of war in English and refers to the Iraqi dictator's 'Arabisation' of the north by ethically cleansing Kurdish villages and towns in eight military campaigns between February and September 1988.

Anfal resulted in the mass executions of Kurdish men and boys of military age, the detention and torture of males aged between seventeen and fifty, the wholesale destruction of thousands of Kurdish villages and the forced displacement of Kurdish villagers to secret locations in Iraq, where many died from malnutrition and disease.

Accounts of the number of dead and the way they died are so emotionally disturbing I can't read them for very long without feeling numb.

Five years before the *Anfal* campaign even started, an earlier act of wickedness against the Kurds was carried out in the Barzan Valley, about an hour's drive due north of Erbil, where I found myself in mountain countryside of staggering beauty.

Towering peaks were dusted with fresh snow; eagles circled lazily in a baby-blue sky and below, the Barzan Valley rolled towards the far horizon like a magnificent emerald carpet.

Bad things didn't happen in such a heavenly spot, did they?

Sadly in Iraq: yes, they did; it's a land where death and human suffering are very much woven into the nation's history.

The deceptively beautiful Barzan Valley is where Saddam Hussein's army committed one of a catalogue of atrocities against the Kurds before the *Anfal* campaign even started.

Legendary, rebel leader General Mustafa Barzani had led a failed Kurdish uprising against the regime in Baghdad and the mountainous region surrounding the Barzan Valley was regarded by Saddam as a hot bed of Kurdish resistance.

Saddam's secret police accused villagers of supplying arms, food and other essentials to Kurdish *peshmerga* fighters holding out in the mountains above. This was probably true, although whether they had any choice in the matter is another story.

One night, in July 1983, the Iraqi Army, supported by the Republican Guard, entered Barzan Valley villages and began rounding up men and boys, aged ten to eighty, all of them members of the Barzani tribe; up to eight thousand total.

An elderly mother called Bahar relived the moment the family's front door was battered down in the early hours: 'It was a horror night for us when the soldiers came,' she said.

'We were asleep in bed when they smashed their way into our home,' she told me.

'They snatched my husband and three sons away. I started screaming, but I was pushed to the ground. They told me my loved ones were being taken away to work as labourers in the south. The soldiers told me they'd bring them back.'

That was a lie. Iraqi soldiers bundled her husband and sons to join thousands of other men and boys from the Barzan Valley, who were herded into trucks and taken to holding centres in Erbil, never to be seen by their loved ones again.

Doctor Bayan Rasul, now a Kurdish psychiatrist, recalled what she saw: 'The buses were big vehicles, each designed to carry about forty passengers,' she said.

'It was really tragic. Fathers, sons and uncles were taken, just the women and children were left behind. The Barzani women never gave up hope their men might return.

They'd been told by government officials the men and boys might come back the next day or in two weeks' time. They were constantly waiting with their eyes fixed on the road,' Doctor Rasul added.

From Erbil, the Barzan Valley men and boys were transported first to the infamous Abu Ghraib prison, twenty miles west of Baghdad, and then to a concentration camp at Bussia, near Iraq's border with Saudi Arabia.

It was there they were shot a hundred at a time and pushed into mass graves, covered with lime and buried under tons of sand.

Saddam Hussein was always very candid about the atrocity and never even tried to cover up.

'The Barzanis spread their treachery... so they've been severely punished and have all gone to hell,' was his justification of the massacre when he met Kurdish leaders in Erbil weeks later.

That was nearly forty years ago, and so far five hundred victims' bodies have been exhumed, identified and returned to the Barzan Valley for reburial. It's very much an ongoing operation.

Bahar, who was in her eighties when I met her recently, is still waiting for the remains of her beloved husband and sons to be returned. As we talked she seemed still traumatised from the night the soldiers came all those decades before and her nut-brown face creased with anguish as she spoke.

'I'm afraid I'm going to die before their bones come back,'

she whispered as tears welled.

'They were innocents, they did nothing wrong, they were killed for nothing,' she said, her voice quivering with emotion.

Her mournful eyes closed, she stopped speaking and I left her overwhelmed with memories.

There can be fewer sadder, heartbreaking places on Earth than the Barzan Valley.

Locals know it by another name: the Valley of Widows.

26. Halabja

Saddam throws a little gas, everyone goes crazy,
'oh he's using gas!'
DONALD TRUMP, DECEMBER 2015

You reach Halabja through miles of pomegranate orchards. When I last visited at the end of 2019, the city was wrapped in glorious sunshine, much like it was when Saddam's warplanes dropped their deadly load of chemical bombs at 11.35 am on March 16th 1988.

'The 16th was a beautiful spring day. The gas that was meant to kill us smelled like sweetened apples,' a Kurdish grandmother told me, as she related her account of that horrific day.

In March 1988 the Iran-Iraq war was stumbling towards a conclusion after eight bloody years in which a million combatants and civilians on either side had lost their lives.

To the surprise of Saddam and his generals, Iran's Revolutionary Guards and their allies, the Kurdish PUK *peshmerga*, made a surprise attack across the border from Iran and routed the Iraqi Army from Halabja.

The Iranians called it Operation *Zafar 7 - Zafar* means victory in Farsi.

The *peshmerga* took control of Halabja city, meanwhile Iranian forces took positions in the mountains surrounding it.

Over a glass of tea I chatted to Rabia, an articulate family matriarch, in her late seventies, who was dressed in black, head-to-toe, including an ebony headscarf.

Recalling March 16th 1988 she said: 'We knew Saddam would be furious his army has been defeated and we had huge feeling of foreboding,' she said.

'The Iraqi Army had already started shelling the town in response.'

She said the family had to make a decision: to flee their home or stay. They decided to remain.

'We felt safer in our homes. We knew if we left at some point we'd run into the Iraqi Army, so better to stay where we were.'

She told me after two days of tension terrible rumours swept Halabja of an imminent gas attack.

'My neighbour warned us he'd heard Saddam had threatened to use chemical weapons,' Rabia continued.

'We were terrified, of course. But, what to do? Our kind neighbour showed me and my husband Mohammed, and our four children, how to place damp towels over our heads in case chemical bombs were dropped.'

Re-living the morning of March 16th she added: 'We heard the thud of bombs being dropped, and after a little while there was a strange smell drifting along our street, like sweetened apples.

That's when we rushed down to the basement of our house. We threw off the damp towels and all of us gathered under a single wet blanket. I remember saying to my husband and children: if we're going to die, we will die together.'

Whilst Rabia's family were cowering in their basement elsewhere in Halabja, thousands of other men, women and children were caught in the open and exposed to clouds of poison gas which seared their lungs.

A Western journalist acquired this graphic eye-witness description:

Children breathed it in greedily, but moments later lay blinded and writhing in their death throes, blood streaming from their eyes, nose and mouth.

In confused agony, they screamed and clawed at their burning skin as it turned red, then black, before they finally fell silent.

An Iranian photographer Kaveh Golestan what he saw, hours afterwards:

It was life frozen. Life had stopped, like watching a film and suddenly it hangs on one frame. It was a new kind of death to me.

The aftermath was worse. Victims were still being brought in. Some villagers came to our chopper. They had fifteen or sixteen beautiful children, begging us to take them to hospital.

So all the press sat there and we were each handed a child to carry. As we took off, fluid came out of my little girl's mouth and she died in my arms.

The bombing by Iraqi warplanes stopped after about five hours and although they still smelled a whiff of gas, Rabia told me she and her family decided to flee their home and head to the Iranian border on foot. It was a journey of only ten miles, but an arduous one, up and down mountain trails.

They joined neighbours making the same journey.

'We took no possessions,' she said.

'We just had the clothes we were wearing. We saw children

wandering around, without parents, that was so sad,' said Rabia.

'We spent the first two nights in caves. And reached the Iranian border and safety on the third day.'

The family remained in Iran for seven months until they felt it safe to return home.

I asked Rabia what her thoughts were on the 30th of December 2006 when she heard the news Saddam Hussein had been hanged, after being convicted of war crimes.

'I would have willingly put the rope around his neck myself,' she said.

As I got up to leave and thanked her for her hospitality, Rabia touched my arm and said, 'Please, make sure you mention the people of Halabja in your book.'

'Every March, on the anniversary of the attack, television crews and journalists, turn up, but they get fewer in number as the years go by. The younger generations have forgotten what happened here. I can understand that, it's a long time ago, but Halabja deserves to be remembered, now and forever.'

At least 5,000 Halabja citizens died from poison gas, with thousands more left horribly injured. Those who perished were buried in mass graves dotted around the city.

The main memorial complex lies on the edge of town and it's dominated by what, to my eyes, is a rather ugly concrete and steel representation of a clenched fist.

When you leave the car park and before the main entrance, the first thing visitors see is a banner which reads: 'Guns are not allowed'.

Parked in a nearby field is a dilapidated Sukhoi war plane which the Kurdish authorities transported from Kirkuk to

Halabja in 2017. It's meant to symbolise the same jet type which bombed the city. A sixty-five-year-old Soviet Tu54 tank, used by the Iraqi Army, sits alongside it.

As you enter the memorial complex, to the right of the main gate, is a striking bronze sculpture of a fallen man trying to protect his son from gas. He's Omar Khawar.

Both Mr Khawar and his son died on March 16th, along with his wife and eight daughters. If the destruction of that family wasn't enough, the memorial curator told me one Halabja family lost thirty three members in the chemical weapons blitz.

The memorial building visitors see today is the second version.

The first was destroyed in 2006 when several thousand angry Halabja residents rioted at the site, setting the original memorial on fire and burning many of its archives; one of the protestors was shot dead by the police and dozens of people were injured.

Locals rioted because they claimed their city urgently needed new roads, hospitals, schools and the Government was accused of using the original memorial site for political purposes.

75,000 citizens of Halabja are still experiencing horrific side effects from chemical weapons, all those years ago, including babies born with deformities and survivors suffering with cancers and breathing difficulties.

Thousands travel to Iran for treatment every year because there aren't sufficient skilled doctors and medical centres in Iraqi Kurdistan.

Halabja survivors, Rabia and her son

Halabja memorial

27. Chemical Ali

Tucked away in a dark corner in the Halabja memorial complex is a macabre exhibit. It's the rope used to hang Saddam's cousin Ali Hassan Al-Majid or 'Chemical Ali,' the man who masterminded the chemical weapons blitz on the city.

Al-Majid was one of the most brutal figures in Saddam's inner circle; a trusted cousin, born in Tikrit in 1939.

In 1988 the Iraqi President handed him sweeping powers to wind up the war with Iran and to defeat the rebellious Kurds - by whatever means.

With some enthusiasm Al Majid called in Iraq's entire military and security services to: 'ban all human existence,' in Kurdish areas - an extension of the *Anfal* campaign.

Al-Majid ordered Iraqi army commanders to:

carry out random bombardments, using artillery, helicopters and aircraft, at all times of the day or night, in order to kill the: 'largest number of persons present,' in what were designated: 'prohibited zones.

One of Al-Majid's directives read:

All persons captured in those villages shall be detained and interrogated by the security services and those between the ages of fifteen and seventy shall be executed after any useful information has been obtained from them, of which we should be duly notified.

But what did chain smoking, pot-bellied, Al-Majid, have against the Kurds?

His hatred seems to have been purely pathological.

The pressure group Human Rights Watch published a 1988 audiotape of meetings Al Majid had with leading Iraqi officials.

In one Al-Majid ranted: 'Why should I let them (the Kurds) live there like donkeys who don't know anything? What did we ever get from them?'

On another occasion, he raged: 'I said: probably we will find some good ones, but we didn't, never.'

On a further tape, he's heard to say: 'I will smash their heads. These kind of dogs, we will crush their heads. Take good care of them? No, I will bury them with bulldozers. I will kill them all with chemical weapons! I'll not attack them with chemicals just one day, but I'll continue to attack them with chemicals for fifteen days.

Who is going to say anything?

The international community? Fuck them...and those who listen to them.'

Fifteen years later, after the US-led invasion of Iraq in 2003, Al-Majid was reportedly killed in a coalition air-strike on a house in Basrah.

In fact, he'd escaped, but was later picked up by the Americans in the same year and put on trial in Baghdad where he was sentenced to death having been found guilty of charges of genocide, war crimes and crimes against humanity.

Al-Majid was hanged in 2010.

28. Hypocrisy

The world found out about Saddam's mustard and nerve gas attack on Halabja after Iran - a country at war with Iraq - spotted a propaganda opportunity and flew Western journalists to the city to film horrific scenes of dead civilians, including children, which littered the streets.

Within hours, news agencies flashed shocking images around the world, prompting an avalanche of condemnation of Saddam Hussein by world leaders, including those in western nations like the United States and Britain.

But who supplied Saddam's regime with the technology and ingredients for chemical weapons used on the Kurds?

None other than those same western powers.

In the mid to late 1980s Saddam was regarded as a US ally and the Reagan administration had removed Iraq from the State Department's list of state sponsors of terrorism, so companies in western nations felt free to supply the Baghdad regime with chemicals, without asking too much about what they might be used for.

Among nations supplying ingredients, or precursors, for chemical weapons were: Singapore (4,515 tons), The Netherlands (4,261 tons), Egypt (2,400 tons), India (2,343 tons), and West Germany (1,027 tons).

Singapore-based firm Kim Al-Khaleej, which was affiliated to the United Arab Emirates, supplied more than 4,500 tons of VX, Sarin and mustard gas precursors and production equipment.

US companies supplying dual use chemicals included Alcolac International, which exported thiodiglycol, a substance which can also be used to make mustard gas.

Few have been arrested and brought to trial for their role in helping arm Saddam's regime with chemical weapons, except, on December 23, 2005, a Dutch court sentenced Frans van Anraat a businessman who bought chemicals on the world market and sold them Baghdad. He was given fifteen years in prison.

The court ruled that the chemical attack on Halabja constituted genocide. Van Anraat was found guilty of 'complicity in war crimes'.

29. Iran accused

A few days after the attack on Halabja, the Reagan administration in the US tried to accuse Iran for the atrocity, even though most world experts and spy agencies agreed Iraqi war planes had been responsible.

The strange move by Washington can only be explained because Saddam was a US regional ally at the time; Iran was America's sworn enemy.

The first notable US figure to point an accusatory finger at Iran was State Department spokesman Charles Redman on March 23, 1988. Later that year, on September 30th, Republican Senator John McCain appeared to make the same accusation.

Both had been referring to a U.S. Defense Intelligence Agency Special Security Office statement compiled after the attack which read:

Most of the casualties in were reportedly caused by cyanogen chlorine.

This agent has never been used by Iraq, but Iran has shown interest in it.

By 2003 Iraq was no longer an American ally and had been cited by President George W. Bush as one of the original members of the so called 'Axis of Evil'. This time the American administration was in no doubt Saddam was responsible for the chemical weapons attack on Halabja and was happy to use it as a *casus belli*.

In his State of the Union speech on January 28th 2003, the President said:

The dictator (Saddam Hussein),who is assembling the world's most dangerous weapons has already used them on whole villages leaving thousands of his own citizens dead, blind, or disfigured.

That should have been the end of any debate, but, three days after the State of the Union, up popped a former CIA intelligence officer, Stephen C. Pelletiere with a surprise op-ed in the New York Times.

Pelletiere wrote:

The accusation that Iraq has used chemical weapons against its citizens is a familiar part of the debate... President Bush himself has cited Iraq's gassing its own people, specifically at Halabja, as a reason to topple Saddam Hussein.

But the truth is, all we know for certain is that Kurds were bombarded with poison gas that day at Halabja. We cannot say with any certainty that Iraqi chemical weapons killed the Kurds.

Pelletier went further and said in any event civilians weren't the principal targets of Saddam's war planes:

This much about the gassing at Halabja we undoubtedly know: it came about in the course of battle between the Iraqis and the Iranians.

Iraq used chemical weapons to kill Iranians who had seized the town, which is in northern Iraq, not far from the Iranian border.

The Kurdish civilians who died had the misfortune to be caught up in that exchange, but they were not Iraq's main target.

Pelletier's op-ed added:

And the story gets murkier: immediately after the battle the United States Defense Intelligence Agency investigated and produced a classified report, which it circulated within the intelligence community on a need-to-know basis. That study asserted that it was Iranian gas that killed the Kurds, not Iraqi gas.

US claims that Iran, not Iraq, bombed Halabja have largely been discredited over the years.

Joost Hiltermann, who was principal researcher for Human Rights Watch between 1992 and 1994 conducted a two-year study of the massacre, including a field investigation in Iraqi Kurdistan.

His analysis of thousands of captured Iraqi secret police documents and declassified U.S. government paperwork, as well as interviews with scores of Kurdish survivors, senior Iraqi defectors, and retired U.S. intelligence officers, confirmed beyond doubt that Iraq carried out the attack on Halabja, and that the United States was fully aware of this, but nevertheless had initially accused Iran, 'for reasons of international politics'.

30. Inside the clan

Despite submitting many requests I never interviewed Saddam Hussein. A handful of Western journalists did sit down with him over the years, but not me.

However, I was in the same room as the Iraqi dictator when his press people invited me and twenty or so journalists to an 'at home' in one of his palaces in Baghdad in the early 1990s.

Amid crystal chandeliers, trays of *canapés* and the murmur of small talk, I sidled up to Saddam who was talking to a Western diplomat. It was 1991 and they were talking about the rebellious Kurds in the north and Shia in the south.

'Listen,' Saddam said to the diplomat, in his rough, working class Arabic.

'The Iraqi people; they're like a young horse.'

The diplomat looked at him puzzled.

Saddam continued: 'Like a young horse, I tell you. Every now and again you've got to hit them very hard on the nose. They won't like it, but they'll know to respect you and keep out of your way.'

How strange those words echoed those of British government officials in the 1920s mentioned in an earlier chapter who spoke about treating the Kurds with: 'a beating one day... and a sugar plum the next'.

Whilst Saddam eluded my attempts to interview him, I did meet and chat on camera with other members of the clan, including the Iraqi President's half-brother Barzan Al-Tikriti.

I'll digress to explain first: who Barzan was and second: how we met and established an odd fellows relationship.

In a classic Saddam family bonding, Saddam and Barzan had the same mother and Barzan's wife and the Iraqi leader's wife were sisters. Barzan's daughter married one of Saddam's sons.

So, the Saddam-Barzan relationship was strong in family terms and for a long time the two men were very close.

From the 1970s Barzan was a member of the Iraqi Intelligence Service and became its director. Saddam appointed him as military governor of Iraq when Shia and Kurdish revolts erupted in early 1991. In those roles, Barzan was directly responsible for the arrest, torture and execution of thousands.

Astonishingly, given his blood-soaked background, he eventually became Iraq's Ambassador to the UN in Geneva and a member of the Human Rights Committee!

And it was while he was in that unlikely role, I put in an interview request in 1993 and found myself invited to his office for coffee and a pre-filming chat.

The address was 28 (a) Chemin du Petit-Saconnex, not the easiest door to find down a lonely side road in Geneva's diplomatic district.

Bizarrely Barzan's office doorbell played the opening bars to the British National Anthem: 'God Save the Queen,' a tune which Americans know as: 'My Country, 'Tis of Thee'.

It wasn't wry Iraqi humour. I found out later that diplomatic staff were unaware of the significance of the doorbell melody.

Smiley, tall and well-groomed in a silk shirt and expensive suit, Barzan, then aged 42, greeted me with the warmest of handshakes. I was struck that he had the same unblinking, dark-eyes as his brother Saddam. It was unnerving; like being stared at by a shark.

He escorted me to his office and a factotum brought sweet tea and a plate of *petit fours*. My host leaned back in his leather swivel chair and relaxed with a Havana.

The first ten minutes was small talk and I had to remind myself the man opposite me had been Saddam's former enforcer in chief.

He was a sadist who tortured and killed for pleasure and renowned for one method of execution: tying his victim to a chair and hammering a nail into the poor devil's skull.

Barzan also had a reputation for offering his torture victims the choice of a swift or slow death at the end of their ordeal.

The former meant a single bullet in the brain.

The latter meant he shot his victim in the arms and legs and then the abdomen, until they eventually bled to death.

Given this brutal background Barzan surprised me somewhat by wanting to discuss the arts. He also seemed to know a lot about western classical music, fine dining and wines.

All very interesting, but eventually I steered the conversation back to his years as head of Iraqi Intelligence and his role in the persecution of rebellious regions like Kurdistan and the thousands of deaths there.

'I know you think I'm a monster,' Barzan said with unexpected frankness.

'All journalists do.'

'But if you do think I'm a bad man, you don't fully understand the mentality of the enemies of my country. Remember John, the men I killed, or had tortured and executed, were killers too. They had to be taught a lesson.'

'Believe me: I have no innocent blood on my hands - none at all,' he said jabbing a finger and leaning his body forward to make a point and encroach on my personal space which unnerved me a little.

We agreed to differ, and moved on to slightly lighter matters like crippling UN sanctions against the regime in Baghdad.

I found Barzan strongly pro-British and, pausing first to a blow a smoke ring from his cigar, he opined: 'Once sanctions are raised there could be oil exploration opportunities for the British in Iraq. I like the British people very much'.

Then he added, with a crocodile smile: 'As Winston Churchill once said, 'You lose friends, but not lasting interests.'

There were some interesting follow-ups to my meeting with Barzan in Geneva, which gave me more insight into the man.

I should make clear to Kurdish friends who lost relatives in the *Anfal* campaign, what follows is no way me being an apologist. Barzan was a butcher and a cruel one at that. But there was another side to his character which ought to be on the record, in my view.

Part of my mission in Geneva was to ask Barzan's help to locate the body of Briton, Doug Croskery, who'd been shot dead by Iraqi soldiers as he tried to escape from Kuwait in the aftermath of an invasion by Saddam's forces in August 1990.

I'd interviewed Doug's wife Thelma in London weeks before and she'd told me how important it was to herself and the family to re-patriate her husband's remains to help them through the grieving process.

Bearing in mind Iraq's border region with Kuwait was littered thousands of human remains and unburied skeletons from the first Gulf War in 1991, it would be a major task locate and identify whatever remained of Mr Croskery.

However, to my surprise, Barzan agreed to help.

I heard nothing for about a year, until a letter arrived for me at Sky News. It was from Barzan.

He explained he'd ordered an elite Iraqi Army unit to look for Doug Croskery's remains, but none had been found. Barzan sent his sincere regrets, which he asked to be passed on the Croskery family.

He added he'd organised the investigation as a personal favour to me and Mrs Croskery and urged me and the Croskery family to keep the matter of his involvement in the search private - 'tell no one' he said.

That year and in the years that followed, Barzan sent me Christmas cards into which he'd folded rambling letters, typed and signed by him. In one, the man who was once Saddam's head torturer wrote:

The importance of human understanding and endeavours is to alleviate even the slightest suffering so that brotherly love, instead of hatred, rancour and bigotry, may prevail.

Indeed, the whole tone of all his correspondence to me over the years was one of implied regret for past misdeeds - without actually saying sorry.

After his wife died from cancer, in 1998, Barzan returned to Baghdad, where he published diaries from his time in Geneva. His meandering journal entries referred to the ideals of Western democracy and women's rights. He stressed the importance of education and wrote:

Education is necessary for all of mankind... even if one does not need education to gain employment, he or she still needs education for its moral and intellectual benefits.

He also wrote about his love for his late wife and his daughters.

At this point it's worth reminding ourselves that the Nazi Party's Josef Goebbels and Heinrich Himmler also left behind journals containing similar sentiments.

Barzan was the 'Five of Clubs' in the famous pack of cards distributed to US troops featuring the fifty-five most-wanted Iraqis following the American led invasion in 2003.

He was picked up by US soldiers following a tip off in April that year and put on trial charged with murder, torture and forced deportation.

Interestingly, he told the judge what he'd said to me in Geneva in 1993 that he thought he had 'no blood on his hands,' although witnesses testified that he shot at will while patrolling the Shia city of Dujail, north of Baghdad, and hanged one woman upside down and tortured her, and munched grapes while administering electric shocks to another.

I was reporting for Fox News from Baghdad in 2007 and Barzan was sitting on death row in a prison about a mile from my camera live-shot position.

One morning I'd heard on a background basis through a US government official that Barzan's execution was imminent, so I had someone from the US State Department deliver a short letter from me thanking him again for organising the search for Doug Croskery's remains back in 1993 and how grateful the Croskery family had been. I thought it was the decent thing to do.

I understand from US officials Barzan received my note and read it, but I never got a reply.

Three days after my memo, on January 15th 2007, both he and Awad al Bandar, one of Saddam's hanging judges, were taken to the scaffold together.

One official present at the execution had a video camera which showed Barzan and Al-Bandar standing side by side facing the scaffold in orange jump suits.

Al-Bandar recited Muslim prayers as executioners placed black hoods over both their heads and looped thick ropes around their necks.

The trap door opened and both men fell simultaneously.

Whilst Bandar's body remained suspended in the air, the rope bearing Barzan snapped back up.

His headless corpse dropped to the floor and his severed head landed and rolled for several feet.

Justice had been meted out to a sadistic brute, but, for what it's worth, I genuinely believe he went to his death a man with remorse for past evil deeds.

31. The King's tomb

We are the descendants of the Medes and Cyaxares
KURDISH NATIONAL ANTHEM

Historians believe the Kurds have their ethnic roots in the Median race, whose most renowned and popular ruler was King Cyaxares (pronounced Kay-Kus-Row)

'King Cyaxares tomb... I want to go,' I said one morning to my fixer, translator, driver and good friend, Karokh Kurdi.

I'd read the burial site had been discovered decades ago and, given his importance to Kurdish heritage, I assumed the father of the nation's grave would be a major shrine and tourist attraction.

Karokh is a savvy, intelligent, twenty-five year-old but to my surprise he was non-plussed.

'John, I'll be honest, I've never heard of the king's tomb being discovered, or even know where it is,' said Karokh.

'We learned nothing about it in school.'

Helpfully, Karokh did a quick ring-around of local journalists in Sulaimaniyah, and they had no clue either.

I wasn't surprised.

On many occasions in the Middle East I've come across a general lack of knowledge or inquisitiveness about ancient history.

In Iraq's case, I find that so ironic.

Iraq is a land rightly described as the cradle of civilisation.

The wheel, writing and algebra were invented there.

The region is mentioned in The Bible's Book of Genesis and it's where formative events in Islam's development unfolded: Ali, the fourth caliph and the Prophet Muhammad's cousin, was murdered at Kufa, and his son Hussein was defeated by Umayyad forces at Karbala.

I can only assume centuries of conflict have made Iraqis more concerned about the here and now rather than developing an interest into what happened at Ur or what ancient characters like Nimrod got up to.

Armed with images I'd downloaded from Google Earth I persuaded a sceptical Karokh that Cyaxares's grave did exist, what's more I had a location.

Showing up on Google Earth on his iPhone was the clincher for young Karokh and we set off in his car for the village of Surdash about 40 miles north of 'Sully'.

We rolled into town in the dusty heat of midday when neither man nor beast stirred, except we found a policeman sitting in the shade outside his station, lovingly cleaning his AK 47.

Like Karokh, the young cop hadn't heard of King Cyaxares's last resting place either, even though we were close, according to Google Earth.

The friendly policeman suggested we set off for caves which he said were a twenty minute drive along a dirt road.

As we meandered through enchanted valleys bounded by honey coloured cliffs the intensity of light was astonishing, similar in quality to the southern Mediterranean in summer.

The track eventually fizzled out to a dead end where we spotted what appeared to be a random set of rickety scaffolding set against a cliff face.

As we closed in on foot, I noticed a makeshift staircase ran up the inside of the scaffolding to a cave about thirty feet off the ground.

Was the cavern the site of King Cyaxeres's tomb? There were no signs or noticeboards to say what we were looking at.

Karokh and I climbed the ramshackle staircase to an open tomb in the cliff face, which I immediately recognised from photographs I'd downloaded from the internet was indeed King Cyaxeres's reputed grave site.

On either side of the tomb entrance were two simple pillars which supported roc friezes of two old men.

From earlier research, I knew the man on the left, who wore a headdress and long sleeved coat similar to the Magi in Biblical stories, was King Cyaxeres. The other, shorter, but similarly dressed man, facing him was a Lydian King: Alyattes.

Above the friezes was a rock medallion with a star symbol which, in King Cyaxeres's time, represented wisdom and fire. The same symbol is now incorporated into the modern-day Kurdish flag.

Just inside the tomb an ante chamber held three empty stone coffins without lids on.

The hills around us were drenched in stillness and for a few moments Karock and I gazed at the vacant coffins mesmerised, taking it all in.

I must say that in the great panoply of ancient burial sites King Cyaxeres's grave is somewhat understated - the Valley of the Kings it is not - but if and when Kurdistan opens up to mass tourism, there will surely be many more thousands climbing the scaffolding.

Who knows? ...the Kurdish Government may even think about opening a visitors' centre.

Our day of discovery wasn't over. We doubled back along the dirt-road, where I'd spotted a direction sign to another cave about 200 feet up the cliff face. The entrance looked, for all the world, like the gaping mouth of a sea monster.

A battered, old sign in English said the cave had been excavated in 1928 by British archaeologist: Dorothy Garrod, whom I later discovered was a 'trailblazing' expert in the Paleolithic period and was the first female professor ever at either Oxford or Cambridge.

My later research revealed the cave was at a settlement known as Zarzi and had been occupied by Neanderthals 32,000 years ago. Subsequent excavations, started by Garrod, found a treasure trove of ancient tools, such as axes and tests on skeletons showed several had been crushed to death in a region prone to earthquakes.

Further laboratory work on relics and animal bones revealed the cave dwellers had killed game such as goats in the valley below and their diet included partridge and duck, as well as freshwater crabs, clams, turtles and fish.

It had been an exhilarating day and as we drove back to 'Sully,' Karokh and I had questions.

Why was the road leading to King Cyaxeres's tomb unmarked and why was a cave, which had rendered up such insight into prehistoric life on Earth, unknown to most Kurds, or indeed the wider world?

'We should know about these things, but our leaders have been more occupied with fighting wars, the last few decades,' said Karokh.

Tomb of King Cyaxeres

King Cyaxeres (left)

32. Bring me the manager

After three decades reporting from Iraq, I know a little about Mesopotamian hotels.

Can I mention Kurdistan notables: the Happy Sleep Hotel, the Hotel Classy; not forgetting Hotel Harem?

And although this book is about the Kurds and their history, I'd like to indulge myself and dedicate a chapter to Baghdad's Al-Rashid Hotel; not only a legend in the hospitality business since 1983, but also a home-from-home for a generation of foreign correspondents covering Iraq's turbulent history, including events in Kurdistan.

The Al-Rashid was unique in so many ways.

Television sets in the bedrooms contained microphones and cameras hidden in them, so Saddam's secret service could spy on guests - for some reason only even numbered rooms.

I know the TV bugging story to be true because I once fled to safety in the hotel's basement during a US missile attack and found myself in a vast rabbit warren of corridors where I saw Saddam's secret police watching banks of monitors which showed some guests still cowering in their rooms through the camera in the TV.

President George H.W. Bush had been US president when American forces ousted occupying Iraqis from Kuwait in 1991. Showing the sole of your shoe to an enemy has long been an insult in the Arab world.

So another Al Rashid eccentricity was a mosaic of Bush's face was set in the entrance to the Al -Rashid's lobby, which guests had to step on to get in.

Beyond the entrance was a long lobby where Iraqi secret police in dark shades and shiny suits lounged on chintzy sofas with bobbles. They pretended to be reading newspapers but were actually keeping a beady eye on who was checking in and out and who was meeting whom in the lobby.

Halfway down the lobby, a pretty, petite Yugoslav young woman - from memory called Katarina - used to tinkle the ivories of a Steinway grand piano. Some days, she'd turn her talents to plucking on an electric harp, twice her size.

The charming young lady's repertoire on either instrument didn't vary much; 'Besame Mucho' and 'Theme from The Deer Hunter,' were two of her staples, whilst sluggish, sloe-eyed waiters wove around her in a desultory fashion serving coffees, teas and stale cakes.

In the early 1990s, the Steinway was blown to pieces in a US Cruise missile strike. The young pianist survived. She'd been sheltering in the same basement I mentioned earlier.

At the far end of the lobby - beyond the lazy waiters, spooks in dark glasses, the tinkling piano and a water feature - was a well-stocked bar, selling counterfeit booze at Manhattan prices to East European arms dealers and... journalists.

I did some of my finest 'doorstep' journalism in the Al-Rashid's lobby; a carousel of notoriety where I grabbed quotes from a mixed bag of visitors over the years, including: the King of Jordan, PLO chief Yasser Arafat, British Prime Minister Edward Heath, UN boss Javier Perez De Cuellar and assorted terror group bad lots like Ahmed Jibril; I even met with boxer and all-round good guy Mohammed Ali.

At the time Ali was in the midst of his battle against Parkinson's Disease and yet he'd pitched up in Baghdad to persuade Saddam to free fifteen American hostages from a General Motors branch who were being used as human shields.

Grinning and very approachable he immediately agreed to an interview, which was a massive honour.

Ali kicked his heels at the Al-Rashid for a week while running out of medication, before Saddam agreed to meet. The boxer returned to the U.S. in December 1990 with the fifteen hostages. The Gulf War started six weeks later.

I can't say the Al-Rashid's accommodation and restaurant facilities lived up the hotel's self-trumpeted, five-star status.

In the early 1990s, myself and other journalists questioned the nature of generous portions of gruel being routinely served up in the restaurant and coffee shop. Giving benefit of the doubt, we assumed it was an exotic Iraqi dish. However, an indiscreet waiter eventually spilled the beans, so to speak.

He whispered we'd been served cattle feed during the previous few weeks because Saddam didn't want us reporting that UN sanctions were making food supplies scarce.

Memorably though, it was at the Al-Rashid I was justifiably on the receiving end of the ultimate angry-guest-put-down from a hotel receptionist.

January 2006 was a bitterly cold month in Baghdad; unusually the city witnessed a few flakes of snow. The Al-Rashid had been without electrical power for two weeks, so there was no heat or lighting in the rooms, no hot water and only cold food in the restaurant.

One freezing morning, like the rest of the guests I'd had enough. No more ice cold showers for me, I thought, so I dried myself off and scuttled down to reception in an ill-fitting dressing gown, flip flops and in high dudgeon.

I thumped on the reception desk and demanded to see the manager.

'Sorry sir, it's not possible,' said the elderly male receptionist, trying to soothe me.

'Of course it's possible,' I retorted. 'I'm a guest here, I'm paying thousands of dollars a month, get me the manager... now!'

'You can't see him sir.'

'Why not?'

'I'm afraid... he's dead,' said the old retainer with what I thought was perhaps a crocodile tear.

'He was murdered last night, shot to death'

Then, without pausing for breath - and here you have to remember we'd had no hot water, lighting or heating for a fortnight and temperatures were sub-zero - I demanded: 'Ok, how about the assistant manager then? Bring him here now, please!'

'Sorry sir, he's dead too. They were both in the same car.'

It was a 'gotcha' moment for the old receptionist and he knew it.

Rightly put in my place I sloped back to my cold room, sat on my bed, pulled on several layers of clothing and boots - and shivered like the rest of the Al Rashid's guests.

I apologised to the receptionist later.

I've had other regular digs in Baghdad, besides the Al-Rashid.

I was on assignment in 2005 for Fox News and joined the network's team bedded down at the Baghdad Sheraton on the east bank of the Tigris River.

The name Sheraton sounds like luxury. It wasn't. The hotel

continued to use the name even though the American parent group had disowned it more than a decade before.

2005 was a difficult year for Baghdad with kidnappings, beheadings and car and truck bombs, all part of a bloody insurgency against an American-led occupation.

Only a skeleton staff of receptionists and maids came to work at the Sheraton every day. The streets were too dangerous for the rest to come to work.

The Fox team were the only guests in the 900 bed hotel - apart from a unit of US special forces who occupied the two top floors.

The presence of the US military made the hotel a regular target for rocket attack and the Sheraton lobby was littered with glass and shrapnel which no one cleared up. Only two of the four perspex bubble lifts worked. The other two had crashed into the lobby and had been left where they fell.

Shia militias used to regularly fire rockets through the gap between the Sheraton and the Palestine Hotel next door at the Green Zone beyond - the rocketeers used to call the hotels the 'goal posts'.

One night, they got their aim wrong and a missile hit the Sheraton killing five.

The battle-scarred hotel caught fire, leaving the Fox team, me included, trapped on the galleried, upper floors.

Looking over the balustrade we watched as enthusiastic members of the Iraqi Fire Brigade did their best to douse the flames eight floors below.

Their corroded fire hoses burst when they tugged too hard on them. Like a comedy scene from the Keystone Cops: the firemen got soaked and the lobby was flooded.

In the end, the fires burned themselves out and we managed to escape to safety down some back stairs.

But, perhaps my lasting memory of the Baghdad Sheraton was one evening when Fox News producer John Terrett and I were both taking the air on the hotel's ground floor terrace, during a pause in daily live shots to New York.

It was sundown, a time when the hotel's murky swimming pool in the terrace area normally filled up with local kids who used it for free to splash around in,

Unusually that evening none of the youngsters showed.

John and I were sitting in plastic chairs near the pool, swapping Fox News gossip, when we both sensed a sudden rush of air and an unearthly whistle. We didn't have time to hit the deck.

A Katyusha rocket whistled just a few feet above our heads, and exploded in an adjoining compound about 400 feet away; home to journalists from the BBC and the Wall Street Journal.

Miraculously, despite the tons of flying concrete and shrapnel, no one was injured.

33. Smugglers' paradise

As a 'veteran' correspondent, I've had to nip, clandestinely, across a few national borders in pursuit of a story.

First time was just before the fall of the Iron Curtain in 1989 when I smuggled myself on false identity papers from West to East Berlin to interview dissidents. I managed to convince border guards at Checkpoint Charlie I was a doctor, not a journalist.

I thought the medical bag and stethoscope had been nice touches.

The Middle East has offered me and camera crews many opportunities for covert crossings.

There's the border between Egypt and the Gaza Strip at Rafa. Above ground are frontier guards, passports checks and customs controls. But, not very far away are underground tunnels used by smugglers to traffic millions of dollars of illicit goods in and out of Egypt every year.

Hard to believe but there used to be a gap in the wall between the Occupied West Bank and Israel, which I filmed near Jerusalem for Al Jazeera news, before the Israelis filled it in.

I can take you to a desolate, border town on the Yemen-Saudi Arabia frontier, where people, drugs and ammunition pass illegally every day through a permanent gap in the razor wire.

And, there's a strip of scrubland on the Iraq-Kuwait frontier at Um Qasir where you don't need passports to cross, if you know and pay the right people.

And I can connect you with Marsh Arab tribal chiefs who'll fix it for traffickers to punt you across vast lakes and past floating border posts into Iran, for fifty bucks, no questions asked.

And then there's Bashmak, which sits on the frontier between Iraqi Kurdistan and Iran.

Bashmak looked like any Kurdish town; the main street was lined with cafes where men sipped tea, gossiped and smoked on hubble-bubble pipes.

Bustling shops sold everything from women's apparel, army boots and socks to kettles, pans, tyres, water pumps and cement mixers.

My team and I – cameraman Feday and producer Seb – were in town to make a film about Kurdish smugglers.

Blacked-out, four-by-fours cruised the main strip where small clusters of men, in woolly, beanie hats, scarves and shades, hogged street corners keeping a watchful eye out for strangers.

Bashmak's streets echoed to the sound of clattering hooves as wiry young men, dressed in dark, baggy pants and tunics whipped emaciated pack-horses and mules into a trot despite being burdened under massive loads covered by plastic sheeting and rope.

In Middle Eastern border towns it's sometimes better to get the lie of the land before setting up a camera and tripod to start filming.

'John, you want me to start rolling and get some shots?' enquired cameraman Feday, who had the good sense to carry his camera by his side, and not on his shoulder, when we first arrived.

'Let's give it a go,' I said, with trepidation.

But it soon became clear in the smuggling town of Bashmak

no one minded being filmed, in fact a scruffy, fifteen-year-old boy approached us and enthusiastically told me his story of how smuggling ran in the family; his father was a smuggler and his grandfather before him; that's why he'd also joined the profession.

The lad ended his on camera interview with an: 'America good!' and a thumbs up, which was his reference to a recent uptick in US sanctions against Iran, which had resulted in Bashmak enjoying a smuggling boon.

Feday finished shooting what are known in television news as general shots/views- visual wallpaper often used at the start of a report to set the scene - and we trudged off to see if we could find some legal trading at the official border post with Iran, half a mile out of town.

The official frontier held no surprises. Beyond a notice, advising you were leaving Kurdistan, there was an up-down barrier, followed by a hundred paces of unkept, no-man's land, before you reached a couple of poles bearing the Iranian flag and a low-rise concrete, customs hall.

Trucks, cars, long distance buses queued to enter and leave Iran, passports were being stamped, fractious kids ran about, a group of travellers were gathered around suitcases rowing with customs officials over something or other – typical of what you might expect.

But on a hill track about half a mile away, we noticed something unusual. From a distance, it looked like a long line of ants.

However, if you squinted hard enough you could see it was actually dozens of men, bent double under heavy boxes strapped to their backs, who were plodding up and over a hill in the general direction of Iran.

All this was in full view of guards at the official border crossing.

We caught up with the 'ant patrol' on the other side of the hillside at what appeared to be base camp where thousands of bottles diesel were stacked in piles. Each pile was guarded by huddles of men and boys who squatted in front of braziers keeping warm.

All around iron-grey clouds hung heavy and low, soldered to the hillside leaving no gap. It was a miserable scene.

'Where's the diesel from?' I asked a young lad with a mop of unruly black hair, heavily calloused hands and a roll-up cigarette dangling from his mouth.

'Iran, mister,' he replied and pointed in the direction of a vast stretch of marshland carved in two by a babbling stream.

There was no fence, barbed wire or anything denoting a frontier but apparently, the fast flowing stream marked the border between Iraq and Iran.

I learned from the young man that he, his brothers and cousins were members of a little cabal who made US$100 running 10-gallon containers of diesel from Iran into Kurdistan every week. It was a family business.

I reminded him border guards were less than half a mile away and could see what was going on.

'Don't border officials come after you?' I asked.

'No,' he said with a chuckle.

'We pay the boss a percentage, so his boys don't cause us trouble.'

If illicit fuel was coming out of Iran, what was going the other way from Kurdistan into the Islamic Republic?

I found the answer in dozens of makeshift tents dotted across the hillside which were packed with electrical goods like refrigerators, washing machines, wide-screen televisions, Play Stations and DVD-players.

They'd been shipped from the Far East into Dubai, then to the Iraqi port of Um Qasir, offloaded into smugglers' trucks and driven north to Bashmak.

En route through Iraq, hundreds of Iraqi and Kurdish highway police would have been paid off to look the other way.

'We're not bad people,' said smuggler Idris, who was in his twenties.

'I smuggle PlayStations into Iran and bring benzine back.'

'We do this because we have no other work in this part of Kurdistan.'

'Yes, it's illegal, but it's the only way I can make any money and feed my wife and kids.'

Elite among Kurdish smugglers are the *kolbars*. Men aged up to seventy and boys as young as fourteen carry mega-weights on their backs up to 150 pounds; one or two told me they could manage just under a quarter of a ton.

We filmed one sinewy fellow in his thirties as he loaded up. First, he stood upright with two ropes slung over his shoulders. His pals then knotted the rope ends around what appeared to be a washing machine covered in Bubble Wrap.

Once the load had been secured the man crouched and then strained like an Olympic weightlifter to heave on the ropes and haul the massive burden on his back.

Bent double by the weight and with his face creased with pain he swayed a little on wobbly legs, but eventually he steadied himself enough to stagger off towards the Iranian border.

It was uncomfortable viewing.

I joined another *kolbar:* a cheerful man in his twenties called Mohammed, who was loaded up with two large-screen televisions.

He set a marching pace as we chatted and descended the hillside towards the Iranian border.

We waded through the foot deep, ice-cold torrent and squelched further through bog-land until after half a mile my cellphone pinged: 'We wish you a pleasant stay in Iran'.

That's when I said farewell to Mohammed and to turn back towards Iraq - I didn't want to be arrested by the Iranians on spying charges.

Mohammed marched on and I watched until he vanished into wisps of mists which drifted across the marshland and the heavily mined region which lay beyond.

Teheran orders regular purges against *kolbars* and Iranian border guards are given standing orders to shoot-to-kill smugglers like Mohammed. In the year we filmed around 150 men and boys out of Bashmak were shot dead during their smuggling mission.

During crackdowns *kolbars* stop using the Bashmak crossing and opt for another route to Iran, further north, across the treacherous Kuh-e-Takht mountain range, which means trekking through at least three-feet of snow in winter where they not only risked being shot, but dozens also perish in avalanches every year.

Human rights groups said the *kolbar* death toll was 232 in 2018 and seventy six in 2019.

If the *kolbars* were the stuff of Kurdish legend, there's another elite group of runners; the smuggling world's special forces.

They're known in Bashmak as the 'Midnight Express'. I wanted to meet them.

Cameraman Feday, producer Seb and I, met Massoud on the edge of town after dark.

The thirty-year-old was happy to talk on camera, but didn't want his face identified, so he wore a black balaclava which showed only his raven-eyes, prominent nose, broad mouth and sallow cheeks.

Massoud told me he was married with two children and three nights a week he and his gang smuggled cigarettes and alcohol into Iran - on horseback.

He explained they were known as the 'The Midnight Express,' because they always set off across the Iranian border in the early hours and rode the mountain trails at a canter.

Massoud beckoned us to follow him to a single storey, breeze-block warehouse where we found the rest of his gang cross legged on carpets warming themselves around a whistling kerosene stove. Wall candles flickered and sent shadows dancing around the room.

On the floor, steam rose from a feast of rice, lamb kebabs, tomatoes, onions, chillies and baskets of *naan* bread.

'We always eat well before a mission,' smiled Massoud.

'We need our energy. Smuggling is hard work and it's cold out there!'

That smoky, whitewashed room was filled with the same badinage I've heard among American soldiers before battle in Iraq. I wondered if the back-slapping and locker room camaraderie belied feelings of nerves?

'How scared are you? ' I asked Massoud.

'Our night journey is very risky. Iranian border guards shoot at us from time to time. One of my friends was shot dead recently, another lost his foot when he stepped on a landmine.'

Massoud was an educated man; the head of the family with responsibilities for his wife and children.

'I went to university and got a degree in law. But there's no work for me, even in cities like Sulaimaniyah,' he said.

'There are no factories in this part of Kurdistan, nothing for us menfolk to do to secure me and my family's future. Yes, I'm scared, but what choice have I got? I've got to earn money somehow.'

We left Massoud and the rest of the gang to dig in to their supper.

Nearby, we found grooms feeding and watering twelve chestnut horses ready for the smuggling mission ahead.

The horses seemed feral and thuggish; their mood was skittish. I noticed a wild look in their dark eyes as they gulped water and oats out of leather buckets, as if they, like their riders, understood there was a perilous mountain journey ahead.

Meanwhile in another small warehouse lit by hissing kerosene lamps, young men busied themselves packing scores of boxes with whiskies like Johnnie Walker, Highland Park Single Malt, Isle of Arran and brandies such as Martell Cognac Special and Hennessy Courvoisier.

It wouldn't be long before this illicit booze would wind up in the homes of well heeled families in north Teheran and members of Iran's theocracy who enjoyed a tipple on the quiet.

It was thirty minutes past twelve when Massoud and the rest of the Midnight Express gang mounted their heavily loaded horses.

I jogged alongside as they left town.

'How much will you make from this trip?'

'About fifty dollars,' said Massoud. 'We get paid when we get to a certain town on the other side.'

'But you might be shot by Iranian border guards.'

'I know, it's a strong chance. I hate this job but, as I told you earlier, I have to feed my wife and kids.'

With that I wished him luck.

A sliver of moon had risen and Massoud and his eleven comrades shrank into the shadow of night, wherein lay Iran.

Months later I read Iranian security forces had captured an alcohol smuggling gang out of Bashmak, and unnamed men had been tried and hanged.

It could easily have been Massoud and other members of the 'Midnight Express'.

I haven't been able to find out.

The next day Feday, producer Seb and I, were leaving Bashmak, but we decided to take one last look at the smugglers' base-camp to film some daytime images in better weather.

We'd stopped our taxi to get the camera out and film, when a Kurdish guy in a Nissan truck, coming the other way, pulled up beside us

'I hope you're making a story about weapons and drugs that cross this border all the time. Big problem,' he shouted leaning out of his truck window.

We'd heard rumours of gun running and heroin trafficking, but during our brief stay in Bashmak we'd found no evidence of either. More time on the ground and perhaps producer Seb and I could have stood the story up.

As a follow up, I read that, in 2019, the Geneva based Global Initiative think-tank made the first major study of illicit trade across Iraq's 900 mile border with Iran, 300 miles of which are in Iraqi Kurdistan, including the smuggling town of Bashmak.

It concluded smugglers were exclusively Kurdish of either Iranian or Iraqi heritage and their activities were 'an open secret and broadly tolerated'.

I could confirm that was not only true, but also the Kurdish forces of law order were complicit.

The report went on to reveal:

The most criminal aspect of smuggling in the region involves the cross-border movement of weapons, narcotics and raw materials for manufacturing drugs, which are smuggled across the Iraq–Iran border using broadly similar methods and routes as deployed for the 'grey' goods supply chain.

Because the same transportation routes and methods for ordinary goods are used to smuggle illegal items, these long-established supply routes enable criminal networks to move contraband with some degree of impunity.

The dossier then quoted one smuggler:

The weirdest thing I carried was Tramadol tablets and battery acid for making drugs like crystal meth.

He went on:

There are a lot of drug laboratories on the Iranian side, close to the border.

Some couriers take raw materials over to Iran and bring back the finished product, although the drugs are also sold inside Iran.

Some couriers also carry opium and a few couriers have become addicts themselves.

The report also looked at the effects of America's re-imposition of sanctions on Iran on 6 August 2018, following the US's pull-out from the 2015 Joint Comprehensive Plan of Action, commonly known as the Iran Nuclear Deal.

The report said:

Two potential unintended, though not unforeseeable, consequences of the re-imposition of US sanctions on Iran are the strengthening of organised criminal involvement, and the fact that smuggling networks may become more focussed in illegal substances such as alcohol, cigarettes, precursor chemicals for drug production and weapons.

34. Komola and Iran's rebellious Kurds

It was well below zero and snowing heavily as our Jeep struggled against the terrain and steepness of the mountain road; the vehicle's chassis creaked as if in pain and our driver cursed the weather as he used a gloved hand to wipe ice from the inside of the windshield.

Cameraman Feday, producer Seb and myself were heading to guerrilla camp in the Zagros mountains, the base of an under-reported Kurdish resistance movement called the Kurdish Communist Party of Iran – or Komola.

The party's base includes Kurdish students, teachers and intellectuals, as well as blue-collar workers and peasants from north western Iran, whose four provinces make up almost ten percent of the population of the Islamic Republic.

In its formative years, Komola was armed and bank-rolled by the former Soviet Union.

By the 1960s, the movement had become a painful thorn in the side of the Shah of Iran and thousands of Komola members were rounded up, tortured and imprisoned at the hands of SAVAK, the notoriously brutal secret police.

When the Shah was toppled in 1979, the persecution of the movement didn't end.

Komola announced it was totally opposed to the rule of the revolutionary regime of Ayatollah Khomeini. He ordered oppression to continue.

Forty years on Iran's Kurdish communities are still persecuted under the regime of President Hassan Rouhani.

State controlled media routinely quotes government officials calling Iranian Kurds 'disobedient'.

So called 'disobedience,' brings consequences.

The Kurdish regions are some of the most economically deprived in the Islamic Republic. Severe poverty in Iran's Kurdish north west has led to social problems, with the region suffering the worst suicide and divorce rates in the whole of Iran.

Drug addiction is also a major issue.

Fifty thousand young Kurds leave provinces like Kermanshah every year to seek work in the central and south of Iran, where they face discrimination finding employment and a place to live.

Against a background of deprivation and discrimination it's no surprise young Iranian Kurds are attracted to movements like Komola – thousands of others have joined jihadi groups in Afghanistan, Iraq and Syria where several currently hold top tier positions in the Sunni HTS militia holding out in Idlib province against Iranian backed forces and Russian airstrikes.

The snowstorm had eased as we pulled up at a wooden barrier at Komola's training camp where armed guerrillas ordered us to step out to be frisked for weapons.

The mountain compound was on the very fringes of Iraqi territory. Iranian frontier guard towers were less than half mile away.

After a rough pat down we were waved inside to make a film report for Al Jazeera News.

The main mess hall buzzed with spirited camaraderie, a

warm fire blazed in a corner and cooks were preparing a meal of rice and lamb and chicken.

Young Iraqi Kurds, both men and women, hugged Iranian comrades who'd made it to the training camp through mine fields and barbed wire on the border.

I got into conversation with one young man called Luqman from Kordestan province in Iran, who was twenty-years old and a student.

'It took me two days trekking through mountains to get here,' he said.

'As well as getting arms training today, I'm also feeding intelligence back on what the mullahs are doing in their persecution of Kurds.'

I asked him for more detail: 'The situation for Kurdish people in Iran is terrible and getting worse.'

'More of my friends have been thrown in jail, some have been executed. Iran is, and always has been, a very dangerous place for us Kurds.'

I asked Luqman about reports that Iranian officials openly distributed heroin to Kurdish youths to get them addicted and less likely to cause trouble for the regime.

'Yes, it's true,' he said. 'They want to turn us into zombies. When we're high, we can't carry out acts of sabotage.'

There was one man in the mess hall in military fatigues who stood out a mile, surrounded by a gaggle of admiring Komola members.

He wasn't young; he was in his mid-fifties, very confidant and jovial and chatted to his young fans in English with a strong American twang.

Israel has always been a solid supporter of the Kurds' struggle for independence and I'd heard reports that retired Israeli special forces officers were training Komola fighters.

He refused to give his name or nationality but he told me he'd be in charge of the live fire training exercise we were about to film.

'Are you Israeli?' I asked.

His tanned faced cracked a smile: 'I'll leave that for you to decide my friend!'

'I'm guessing you are,' I said.

'I can't confirm or deny,' he replied with a chuckle.

He then turned to the rest of the room and yelled, 'Come on guys, let's go.'

'Let's kick butt!'

With that the mystery commander - I had no doubt he was Israeli - led some fifty or so Komola guerrillas out of the camp and up a mountain trail like the Pied Piper of Hamelin.

My cameraman Feday, producer Seb and I followed in their wake.

The Zagros mountains, held a rare magnificence and as we climbed higher we found ourselves in a place of hypnotic beauty.

The earlier snowstorm had passed and the sky was both blue and gin-clear. Around us, peaks glistened with powdery, champagne snow which glittered in the afternoon sun.

Over my right shoulder: the Iranian border. Over my left: Turkey, and behind me: I could just pick out tall buildings in Sulaimaniyah, miles away on the blurred horizon.

It was difficult to keep pace with the Pied Piper and his young followers who marched ever upwards with great lolloping strides common to mountain people.

By the time we reached the mock battle area early arrivals had already started launching rockets at the wreck of a truck about a two hundred yards away.

As explosions and gunfire echoed around the mountains Seb and I sheltered behind a giant boulder as Feday filmed from a safe vantage point.

Someone loaned me binoculars. I focussed on an Iranian frontier tower close by where I spotted the Islamic Republic's border guards taking a peek back at us!

I suddenly realised the live fire exercise was meant to send an important message to Teheran.

Later in the afternoon I sat down with Komola's Secretary General, Abdullah Mohtadi, a quietly spoken, middle-aged man with a softly aquiline nose, who could easily have passed muster as an accountant or bank manager - not the leader of a fanatical guerrilla movement.

At the time of our conversation, Komola had joined a loose association with other Iranian Kurdish rebel factions, but were still searching for a single vision or roadmap to pursue together.

It seemed they were struggling with the age old curse of Kurdish disunity.

'We've had our difficulties but I think we're heading to being united now,' said Mohtadi, perhaps more in hope.

Komola itself had splintered on several occasions and in the mid-1980s, hundreds died in fighting between Komola and another Iranian Kurdish group the KDPI.

Back on firmer ideological territory, he went on, 'Discrimination against the Kurds in Iran is so deeply embedded, it's the norm, and I want you to tell the world that. We must force the Iranian government to respect the Kurdish people.'

The Iranian Government's current policy towards all Kurdish opposition groups, including Komola, is that they are enemies of the state - pure and simple.

Iranian Kurdish leaders claim at least eight activists are shot every week by Iranian police or Revolutionary Guard members.

'They have a shoot-to-kill policy and use it with impunity,' Mohtadi told me.

At the time of writing the abuse of Kurdish human rights in Iran continues, despite international condemnation, and pressure groups like Amnesty International and Human Rights Watch list dozens of persecution cases.

In 2009, Amnesty drew attention to the case of Ehsan Fatahlan a twenty-eight year old Kurd, accused by Teheran of 'propaganda activities against the regime,' and of helping the Kurdish resistance group Komola.

He was originally sentenced to ten years, but later changed to death by hanging.

Referring to this and other executions of Kurdish men and women, Human Rights Watch reported in 2019:

The execution numbers today are very alarming.
We are faced with a new wave of violence by the Iranian government which is only comparable to the early days after the revolution.

A year after Iran executed Ehsan Fatahlan, a second Kurdish political prisoner, Fasih Yasamani was put on trial for 'enmity against God'.

Like Fatahlan, Yasamani, a twenty-seven-year-old father of two, was tortured as authorities tried to force him to confess, but he refused. They still hanged him.

In 2018, a Kurdish human rights group reported thirteen Kurdish men and women had been executed for what was described by the Iranian government as 'political and religious activities'.

The same year Iran announced it had executed three Iranian Kurds accused of belonging to Komola, for taking part 'in attacks against civilians and security forces in western Iran'.

All recent execution of Kurds took place despite calls for clemency by UN human rights special rapporteurs Javaid Rehman and Agnes Callamard, who said the accused men hadn't been given a fair trial.

35. Khalkhali: the hanging judge

He was a short, rotund Iranian cleric, with a pointed beard and an assassin's smile; friends and enemies remember his weird, high-pitched giggle. Ayatollah Sadegh Khalkhali had a pathological hatred of Kurds.

In the febrile days immediately after the Islamic Revolution in 1979, which swept the Shah from power, the country's new leader, Ayatollah Khomeini, appointed Khalkhali as chief justice of the revolutionary court system - a role he accepted with relish.

Khalkhali immediately declared every Iranian citizen had the right to be an executioner and he told the 'children of the revolution,' to 'dispense with troublesome formalities,' like a formal arrest and trial.

Under Khalkhaki's watch dozens of gallows were hitched up in Teheran's main streets and so called 'enemies of the revolution' were hanged - sometimes eight at a time.

Khalkhali's fearsome reputation reached another level when he was put in charge of trying the Shah's former Prime Minister Amir Hoveida.

It was nothing more than a show trial and having been found guilty of sedition, corruption, espionage and fourteen other trumped up charges, Hoveida was marched out of court and shot by a firing squad. Khalkhali watched the execution and some reports said he even fired one of the guns.

Hanging judge Khalkhali had a particular hatred of Kurds

and when Kurdish revolts flared in the early days of the Islamic Republic he showed no mercy.

His record of hanging more Kurds than any other judge has yet to be broken.

In his book he wrote:

I killed over 500 criminals close to the royal family, hundreds of rebels of Kurdistan, Gonbad and Khuzestan regions, and many drug smugglers.

I feel no regret or guilt over the executions. Yet I think I killed little. There were many more who deserved to be killed but I could not get my hands on them.

Before Khalkhali was forced to resign, in an embezzlement scandal, involving US$14 million, he was said to have condemned 8,000 men and women to death.

Many of them were Kurds whom he machine gunned to death himself.

He once told an interviewer from the French newspaper Le Figaro, 'if my victims were to come back to Earth, I would execute them again, without exception.'

In 2003 Khalkhali died from cancer and heart disease, aged 77.

36. Four empty graves

Iraqi Kurdish politics has been predominantly secular, but that's not to say radical Islam hasn't found a foothold in Kurdistan.

Around a thousand Kurds had joined the Islamic State movement by the time the jihadists reached peak strength in 2014 - disillusionment with politics and persuasive radical clerics were instrumental in recruitment.

Prior to that, home-grown Kurdish jihadi groups have mostly been splinters of the Islamic Movement of Kurdistan, the IMK, founded in 1987 by Iran backed Sheikh Uthman Abdul Aziz.

The IMK itself disarmed seventeen years ago and hasn't participated in Kurdish politics in any observable way since 2013, but one of its significant, radical offshoots was called: Ansar Al-Islam (The Partisans of Islam)

Ansar was a surrogate of Osama Bin Laden's Al Qaeda.

Middle East watchers were taken aback when Ansar, unexpectedly, established a mini Islamic state centered around the town of Biyara in south east Kurdistan, close to the Iranian border.

It was the first time Kurdish jihadists had been able to control a swathe of territory and rule it based on a strict interpretation of Sharia law, a rite of passage towards the realisation of the ultimate goal of an Islamic caliphate.

They'd been helped by Iranian Kurds who provided vital cross-border assistance with food and supplies and crucially facilitating passage for foreign fighters who wanted to join. These included several hundred Saudi Arabian, Iraqi, Syrian, Palestinian, and Jordanian jihadis who were smuggled in to join the cause.

Before the US-led invasion of Iraq in 2003, four members of Ansar murdered Franso Hairiri, a senior official of Kurdistan's KDP party as he travelled to work in Erbil in 2001.

In the same year Ansar jihadists killed more than fifty *peshmerga* militia aligned to the PUK party; most were beheaded.

A year later they attempted to assassinate the then PUK leader Barham Saleh - who's currently Iraq's President. He survived, but five of his bodyguards died.

Ansar sprang to prominence on the world stage on February 5th 2003, when US Secretary of State Colin Powell made a presentation to the UN Security Council.

Powell was making a case to justify an American-led invasion to topple Saddam Hussein and claimed Ansar had, with the Iraqi leader's approval, established a 'poison and explosive training centre camp,' in Kurdistan.

Based on Powell's evidence, the American military launched an assault on Biyara and surrounding areas firing around fifty Tomahawk cruise missiles. US special forces and Kurdish *peshmerga* fighters also took part in the attack.

The Pentagon estimated 250 out 700 Ansar fighters had been killed and US officials claimed the movement's leadership were wiped out when their headquarters in Biyara, was bombed.

I was sent to Biyara by the Al Jazeera news desk to investigate Pentagon's claims.

A concrete office building in the middle of Biyara had been

flattened by a 5000-pound American missile which had blasted a massive hole in the flat roof.

It was late afternoon a couple of days after the US blitz and locals, some with babies and bags of shopping, picked their way over great chunks of rock and twisted metal- all that was left of Ansar's headquarters.

Through an interpreter I asked one old man what life had been like under Ansar's Sharia regime.

He told me the town's menfolk had been ordered to grow their beards longer to the size of two fists. He said women and girls weren't allowed to work or attend school and no one was permitted to smoke, listen to music or watch television.

He also said men guilty of theft had their right hands chopped off. Anyone found drinking alcohol was flogged and adulterers were stoned to death.

'Life was very, very bad,' said the grizzled old man with some understatement.

He went on: 'One jihadi overheard my son listening to music on his CD player in his bedroom. They took him away and tortured him.'

At that point tears welled in the old man's eyes.

He continued: 'My son was a changed boy after that. He still has nightmares.'

I asked local people to confirm the Pentagon's claim Ansar's leadership had been killed in the American air strike.

They said they didn't know but after we finished filming a middle aged fellow tugged on my sleeve and insisted we accompany him. He pointed up to the mountains which towered above Biyara.

He clearly wanted to show us something. He said he had a car and he'd take us.

About thirty minutes later cameraman Feday, producer Seb and I found ourselves on winding mountain paths where shepherds tending sheep were settling down in tents just as the sun slid beneath distant peaks.

The man tugged on my arm and led us to four empty holes in the ground, about six feet deep.

In broken English he said they were graves dug by four members of Ansar's leadership who wanted to be buried there if they were killed.

On the journey back down from the mountain, two thoughts struck me.

First: if Ansar's leadership had dug their own graves, had they been tipped off about an American air attack.

Second: the graves were empty so the leadership probably hadn't been killed, as the Pentagon claimed.

I was able to pursue the story the following day.

I got consent to film in a high security jail in Sulaimaniyah and interview a senior member of Ansar who'd been had been captured after the US rocket attack.

Guards brought in a handcuffed man in his late twenties. He was well built, his eyes were the shape of almonds and his jet black hair had been tied into a top knot. He wore a red, checked shirt and scruffy blue jeans.

He said he was Iraqi, his name was Abdul Rahman and he confirmed he was a senior member of Ansar.

I should point out there were also three other men in the tiny room which had a table and half a dozen chairs.

I assumed they were Kurdish intelligence officers. One of

them took notes of my interview with Rahman.

After a firm handshake, Rahman, who had good English, explained the mystery of why the graves we'd seen in the mountains outside Biyara, were empty

'Yes, we were tipped off about the American Cruise missile attack,' he said with a satisfied smile.

'I can't tell you how we knew, but we learned an hour before the US rockets fell that we were going to get hit. It was a good tip off and we got out of our headquarters in time - that's the leaders, myself and dozens of comrades. The Americans had bombed an empty building. They claimed they killed our leadership. But it wasn't true.

The leadership escaped, that's all I can tell you.'

I asked Rahman what links Ansar had with Al Qaeda and Saddam Hussein, in the light of Colin Powell's claims in the UN.

Rahman confirmed he and fellow fighters had undergone training in Al Qaeda camps in Afghanistan.

'But, we had absolutely no connection with Saddam,' he insisted.

'I would tell you if we had. We supported Saddam, but he gave us no help, either with weapons or money. Also we had no chemicals or poisons of any kind, so what Colin Powell told the UN was false,' he added.

So, why did the Kurdish authorities allow me to interview a high profile prisoner like Rahman, a key member of the Ansar movement?

Maybe to set the record straight and send a message to the Americans that Ansar were still around and a threat?

I never found out, and years later I heard Rahman had been

killed in fighting in Iraq, so he must have been freed some time after we'd sat down together.

Meanwhile what had actually happened to Ansar's leadership and rank and file members who'd occupied and terrorised the town of Biyara?

I learned later from Kurdish officials that with Teheran's approval Ansar members had crossed the border to the Iranian city of Mariwan where they were given new homes on the edge of town.

They were warned by the Iranian authorities to keep a low profile and that they'd be deported back to Iraq if they started gathering in groups.

On August 29th, 2014 the Ansar movement announced it had merged with Islamic State which had already set up a so-called 'caliphate' including wide swathes of Iraq and Syria.

Interestingly, the most recent Islamic movement to declare itself in Kurdistan, was in 2017. They called themselves the White Flags and were led by a one-eyed, middle-aged former Al Qaeda in Iraq member called Hiwa Chor.

The group claimed to have carried out attacks on Kurdish oil-pipelines to Turkey.

A Kurdish Government spokesman insisted White Flags were actually a front organisation for Ansar Al-Islam.

37. Mahabad

Journalists often trot out a line that the Kurds have never had their own country - 'a people without a state,' is how they're often described.

I've fallen for the same cliche myself.

But over seventy years ago, Kurds did have their own nation - for just shy of twelve months.

It was called Mahabad.

I passed through the city of Mahabad, in north west Iran, some years ago whilst researching an article about British explorer, Dame Freya Stark.

La Stark had been in the region in the 1930s searching for the Ashafin tribe and you can read about her expedition in her book: Valleys of the Assassins.

The city's zenith was during the first millennium BC, when it was at the heart of the Mannaean civilisation - a race renowned for horsemanship and agricultural skills.

Nowadays, some of Mahabad's population of 200,000 are more likely to have jobs in, or connected to, Iran's petrochemical industry, which is very much integral to life there.

I was in Mahabad, where they speak the purest form of Kurdish, for only a day and a night.

I recall the city being shrouded in freezing fog and remember a kind mullah who gave me a lift from the bus station to my modest hotel in his Soviet version of an American Jeep, left over from the Second World War, called a GAZ 67.

And there's the link to this story.

The Soviets brought plenty of GAZ 67s to Mahabad and the rest of what was then Persia in August 1941 when they and the British Army invaded and ousted the pro-Nazi leader Reza Shah and replaced him with his more compliant son Mohammed.

Persia's Kurds welcomed the invasion. It meant an end to persecution by the Shah's regime.

For a snapshot of Kurdish daily life pre-invasion, I turned to a French made documentary.

Film-makers had interviewed an eighty-five-year-old Kurd, called Hashem Barza, who recalled daily life.

'The Kurds suffered very badly,' he said.

'The Kurdish language was banned in schools and in legal proceedings. Only Persian was allowed.'

In the same film, an elderly woman, Kobra Azimi said:

'The Iranians thought the Kurds were vermin and shouldn't even exist. It was particularly bad for Kurdish men. If they wore their traditional baggy Kurdish trousers the Shah's police would arrest them in the street and cut the crotch out of the pants with a knife. The men were made to feel totally humiliated and helpless,' she added tearfully.

After the invasion came another pivotal moment for the Kurds. Soviet leader Joseph Stalin declared north west Persia, including Mahabad, would be annexed and attached to the Soviet Union.

Kurdish nationalists seized their chance and became more active.

Schools started to teach Kurdish as well as Persian. There were no text books in Kurdish, so teachers used Kurdish language newspapers printed outside Iran, for pupils to study.

Shaleel Ghadani was just a boy when he attended Kurdish lessons.

He told the documentary makers: 'At first we were taught in secret and at night, but then teachers got more bold and Kurdish lessons were openly accepted.'

'It was very exciting!'

During this period of relative freedom left-wing Kurds got together and formed their own political party, the Kurdistan Democratic Party of Iran, which was set up in Mahabad, headed by: Qazi Mohammed.

'Qazi Mohammed was a well-known judge. His family had been part of the judiciary in Mahabad for three hundred years,' Hashem Barza, a close family friend recalled.

'Qazi Mohammed was well respected. He spoke many languages: Kurdish, Persian, Turkish, Arabic, French, German some Russian.'

'He was sophisticated, hugely likeable. People loved him,' added Hashem.

With the backing of supporters Qazi Mohammed created the Kurdish People's Government of Mahabad on December 15th 1945.

He was made President and on January 22nd 1946 he climbed to the top of a government building in Mahabad's main square and declared the Kurdish Republic of Mahabad, territory which also included the neighbouring towns of Bukan, Piranshahr, Sardasht and Oshnavieh.

For some months the Kurdish Republic of Mahabad was politically stable based on a constitution which included: autonomy for Iranian Kurds, the use of Kurdish in schools and a requirement all state officials had to be Kurds.

Whilst the new republic had an army, a constitution, a seat of power and a president, it lacked a flag.

Qazi Mohammed turned to the daughter of a family friend, Fatima Shahin and asked: 'Could she make a flag?'

'Why not, just give me the pattern, and tell me the colours and the shape,' responded Fatima, who was only fourteen at the time.

Young Fatima created a flag with horizontal bars of red, white and green and a sun symbol in the middle with twenty-one rays representing Nowruz, a holy day in March marking the vernal equinox or new beginning.

She wouldn't have known it then but she'd sewn, arguably, the most important and iconic symbol of Kurdistan ever.

Documentary makers interviewed Hashem who recalled the first time the new flag was raised in Mahabad.

'The rooftops surrounding the square were packed with people. Qazi Mohammed arrived and we all started applauding,' he said.

'Everyone clapped along as we sang our national anthem. Qazi swore an oath on the Koran to Kurdistan and to the flag and to national honour. He swore devotion to the Kurdish struggle and the Republic, until death. That was the most memorable day, in all my years. I'll never forget it. Even now that memory ignites a passion in me.'

A newly independent Mahabad soon began attracting Kurds from Kurdish regions in Iraq, Syria and Turkey including Mustapha Barzani, the most powerful leader of Iraq's Kurds. He crossed the Zagros mountains to join Qazi Mohammed in Mahabad, with 1,500 fighting men.

Qazi Mohammed made Barzani a senior general and his force became the backbone of the Mahabad army, then 13,000 strong.

But, no story about the Kurds and independence was going to end well. International *realpolitik* intervened once again, as it had after the First World War.

At the Yalta Conference in February 1945, Winston Churchill, Franklin D. Roosevelt and Joseph Stalin agreed the Soviets and British would withdraw their troops from Iran and sovereignty over north-west Persia, including Mahabad, would be restored to the Shah.

As soon as the conference accord was signed the fledging Kurdish nation was doomed.

Without Soviet military protection and economic support President Qazi Mohammed and Mahabad's Kurds were left to fend for themselves against the Persian Army.

Kurdish tribal leaders, who'd flocked to Mahabad from countries including Turkey in the heady days of independence, began to desert and head home.

Fatima Shahin recalled: 'Many sold out. Only the Barzani men stayed loyal to Qazi Mohammed.'

But, in the end, even Mustapha Barzani called an urgent meeting with Qazi Mohammed to tell him that with great pain in his heart he too would be making a break for the safety of the Soviet Union, with 500 of his men.

At a moving final meeting of the two men, Barzani suggested Qazi Mohammed should leave with him.

'Qazi told Barzani, I'm not coming with you,' recalled the President's bodyguard, Bedew, who was a witness to the conversation.

'I've brought this on my people and they will say I have abandoned them, if I go. Therefore, I must stay here in Mahabad.'

Then, according to Bedew, the President made a parting request to Barzani: 'Take the Kurdish flag with you, as you go.'

'Qazi then pulled it from his pocket and handed it over to Barzani.'

In an emotional scene Qazi Mohammed began to cry and Barzani also sobbed as he and his men headed to a mountain track out of Persia and into the Soviet Union.

Inevitably, Persian troops overran Mahabad in December 1946.

Having got what he thought was an amnesty from Teheran, President Qazi Mohammed handed himself over to Persian security services, who arrested him and charged with being a Soviet spy.

There was a secret trial in January 1947 and two months later, on March 31st that year, Qazi Mohammed, the founder of the first independent Kurdish state was hanged in Mahabad's town square, along with his brother and cousin.

'God, who had given us so much happiness suddenly took it away,' said Fatima, who as a girl, had sewn the original Kurdish flag.

Mustapha Barzani successfully reached the Soviet Union with his fighters, where he lived in exile for eleven years before returning Iraq.

As leader of the KDP party he became one of the most prominent figures in Kurdish politics and led the Kurds in revolution against the Arab regime in Baghdad.

He died from cancer in a Washington DC hospital in 1979.

His son Masoud Barzani became President of the Iraqi

Kurdistan region, until his mandate expired in 2015.

Although the Republic of Mahabad lasted for just less than a year the extraordinary story of its creation and the bravery of Mohammed Qazim remains an inspiration for many Kurds.

Copies of the distinctive Kurdish flag designed by Fatima Shahin, who died in Erbil in July 2012, flies from every public building across the region.

38. By the rivers of Babylon

By the rivers of Babylon we sat and wept
when we remembered Zion.
There on the poplars
we hung our harps,
for there our captors asked us for songs,
our tormentors demanded songs of joy;
they said, 'Sing us one of the songs of Zion!'
How can we sing the songs of the Lord
while in a foreign land?
If I forget you, Jerusalem,
may my right hand forget its skill.
May my tongue cling to the roof of my mouth
if I do not remember you,
if I do not consider Jerusalem
my highest joy.
Remember, Lord, what the Edomites did
on the day Jerusalem fell.
'Tear it down,' they cried,
'tear it down to its foundations!'
Daughter Babylon, doomed to destruction,
happy is the one who repays you
according to what you have done to us.
Happy is the one who seizes your infants
and dashes them against the rocks.

PSALM 137

We heard in a previous chapter the Christian community faces extinction in Iraq. But another religious sect has already disappeared.

As I've gone about my journalistic assignments in Iraq I've spotted remnants of the lost tribe; crumbling synagogues, door lintels engraved with Hebrew writings - but that's all.

Just ruins, nothing more.

Jewish history in Mesopotamia began when King Nebuchadnezzar sacked Jerusalem in around 600 BC and deported thousands of Jews to what was then Babylon.

Three more mass deportations followed, including thousands of priests, scribes, farmers, shepherds and artisans.

The original deportees brought in their extended family members until there were Jewish communities far beyond Babylon, including in Kurdish cities like Dohuk and Erbil, where Jewish neighbourhoods clustered around what was often called: 'Jew Street'.

Babylon, a thriving city sixty-miles, south of Baghdad, became a world centre for Judaism and at the peak of power and influence - around four hundred years or so before the birth of Christ - a third of Baghdad's population were Jewish.

Across the centuries, successive conquerors, including the Mongols and the Ottomans, persecuted Mesopotamia's Jewish population and by mid-Victorian times travellers reported Baghdad's Jewish population, most of whom worked in government jobs, had fallen to just 16,000.

The 1930s saw a massive rise in anti-Jewish sentiment, not only in Europe, but the same anti-Semitism also to spread to Iraq.

Baghdad and Erbil witnessed pogroms and hundreds of Jews

were thrown in jail, whilst others were dismissed from the army and government positions.

On 1st June 1941, a Nazi-inspired pogrom erupted in Baghdad, bringing to an end more than two millennia of peaceful existence for the city's Jewish minority.

Thousands of armed Iraqi Muslims went on the rampage, with swords, knives and guns. The official death toll of Jews was 180 but some historians believe as many as 600 died.

'On the first night of Shavuot we'd usually go to a synagogue and stay up all night studying the Torah,' said Haddad, now a veteran ophthalmologist in New York.

'Suddenly we heard screams: 'Allah Allah! and shots were fired. We went out to the roof to see what's happening, we saw fires, we saw people on the roofs in the ghetto screaming, begging God to help them.'

In a tragic twist, it turned out the British Army could have intervened to halt the violence. On the day of the pogrom the British cavalry were just eight miles from Baghdad, having raced 600 miles from Palestine and Egypt under orders to prevent Iraqi oil falling into Nazi hands.

'To Britain's shame, the army was stood down,' said historian Tony Rocca, co-author with survivor Violette Samash in the book, Memories of Eden.

Rocca added: 'Sir Kinahan Cornwallis, Britain's ambassador in Baghdad, for reasons of his own, held our forces at bay in direct insubordination to express orders from Winston Churchill that they should take the city and secure its safety. Instead, Sir Kinahan went back to his residence had a candle-light dinner and played a game of bridge.'

During those turbulent days Erbil's persecuted Jewish

families fled other pogroms to make new homes in Singapore, where they'd already established trade ties - Singapore's Jews number around 10,000 today, with most tracing their roots to Iraqi Kurdistan.

In September 1948, one of Iraq's richest Jews, Shafiq Adas, was publicly hanged outside his house in Basrah on what were thought to be trumped up charges of selling scrap metal to the fledgling state of Israel.

Two years later, against a background of anti-Jewish sentiment, the Iraqi Parliament passed a law 'allowing' Iraqi Jews to leave the country for good, as long as they renounced their citizenship and gave up their property including their bank accounts.

Approximately 100,000 departed Iraq for Israel.

About 6,000 decided to stay, but numbers fell further and, by the time the Baath Party came to power in 1968, there were approximately only 2000 Jews left in Iraq.

Under Saddam's rule the dwindling Jewish communities again suffered severe persecution and discrimination.

His government warned the public not to co-operate with Jews and Jewish business licenses to trade were taken away.

Morris Zebaida, a survivor who now lives in London, said: 'We learnt to live like mice. If we didn't, we would be spat upon or arrested.'

Between January 1969 and January 1970, thirteen Iraqi Jews were convicted on spurious charges and were hanged. By 1973 a further forty-six were either executed, kidnapped or simply disappeared, presumed murdered.

Sources in Israel reported that in 1996, there were just 120 Jews living in Iraq and 'probably' none today.

But was that the end of the story? Had all the Jews really quit Iraq? Maybe some had returned, especially as Israel has close ties with the Kurdish Government in Erbil.

In the absence of any leads, finding a functioning synagogue seemed like a reasonable starting point.

During reporting assignments in the 1990s and the 2000s to Baghdad and cities in the south, such as Najaf and Basrah, I asked around local journalistic contacts and was told there were no synagogues left intact - they'd either collapsed through neglect, been demolished or destroyed during decades of conflict.

In 2015, as part of my ongoing search, I came across one or two abandoned and dilapidated cottages close to the Citadel in Erbil. They had Hebrew inscriptions across the door lintels.

One of the crumbling buildings could even have been a small synagogue, but the roof looked like it could collapse at any time and I didn't try to enter to investigate further. I asked around but there were definitely no Jewish families in the neighbourhood.

During my last visit to Erbil, in late 2019, even those remnants of Jewish life had been demolished and the rubble cleared.

I also visited Dohuk to try to find Jew Street, but locals I spoke to hadn't heard of it and I wasn't able to find it on my own. Maybe it's been renamed. Perhaps it no longer exists.

Of course, synagogues aren't the only evidence of a Jewish presence. What about religious shrines?

Looking for evidence of shrines to Judaism in Iraq was equally frustrating, partly because the waters have been muddied by Islam having embraced the major Hebrew prophets.

Also, Islamic State fighters have destroyed so many ancient sites including Jonah's tomb, near Mosul, in 2014; the jihadists also dynamited a leading synagogue in Mosul which lies in ruins.

The closest I ever came to finding any intact shrine with links to Judaism was while researching the prophet Ezra.

He was a significant Babylonian Jew and was buried seventy miles north of Basrah at Uzair.

His tomb was also dynamited by Islamic State, but near a busy dual carriageway in the west of Erbil, there's a monument to Ezra in the form of a 100 feet tall minaret with a high octagonal base and tall shaft.

Even that wasn't built by Jews but by Muslim artisans around 1,200 AD. Today it leans like the Tower of Pisa, with part of the tower section missing.

The shrine complex was closed to visitors when I called in, however the city council had planted a pleasant park around it and it's a place where families enjoyed picnics.

I feel confident in saying that monument to Ezra is probably the only intact shrine with any links to Judaism in the whole of Iraqi Kurdistan - it's certainly the tallest.

Ideally, I wanted to find some Jewish families; stragglers left behind from the great Jewish exodus of the early 1950s, or perhaps returnees from Israel.

After a few phone calls to journalists in Erbil and Dohuk I soon realised I was chasing ghosts until, by chance, I saw an advertisement in a Kurdish newspaper for a lecture at Erbil's Kurdistan University, by a young American Jew: Levi Clancy.

The college is a stone's throw from Ezra's shrine and after submitting a copy of my passport and my press pass in advance,

I received an invite.

The audience included about thirty men and women of all ages. I guessed, from their general facial appearance, they had Jewish ancestors.

Levi was an engaging, bright-eyed twenty something from New York, who wore a *yarmulke* and revealed he'd lived as a student in Erbil for five years.

He spoke passionately about Jewish history in Mesopotamia and when I asked were there any Jews left in Iraq his reply answered all my questions.

He told me several hundreds of Jews who'd chosen to remain after the mass expulsion in 1950 had converted to Islam, for the purely practical reason of enjoying a better life, free from persecution.

Their modern-day relatives had adopted the Muslim faith and were known in Kurdistan as *Ben Jews* or sons and daughters of Jews.

Levi said they had a pride in their heritage, although any links to Judaism was more to do with the blood connection, rather than their observance of a religious creed.

He added: 'Thousands of *Ben Jews* live here in Kurdistan and they're proud of the fact they have a Jewish grandmother or grandfather, but they can't practice their ancestors' faith because there's no where to pray - even if they wanted to.'

I asked him whether any of Kurdistan's Jews, who fled in the early 1950s, had returned to cities Erbil?

'Maybe a handful in the early days, but they went back to Israel eventually,' he said.

'Jewish families in Israel, with links to Iraq may want to travel to the home of their ancestors, but they'll never return.

They're too afraid.'

Levi told us he'd lived openly as a Jew in Iraqi Kurdistan for five years. I asked if he'd ever been the subject of abuse or discrimination?

'No direct physical or verbal abuse. It's more subtle. Conspiracy theories about Jews are still rife here. I'll give you an example,' he said.

'I was in a car with a Kurdish friend and we were stopped at a check-point for an ID check. I showed my student card to the policeman and not my ID card. The policeman just glanced at the student card, didn't demand my ID, and waved me and my friend on. As we drove away my friend turned to me and got angry.

He demanded to know why I'd been let off with showing my student card rather than my formal identity card, implying that I, as a Jew, had got a special favour from the police. Isn't it strange, the suspicion about a Jewish conspiracy is always there?'

I was grateful I'd met Levi.

He'd convinced me there were no Jews native to Iraq living in Iraq nowadays, but the presence of hundreds of *Ben Jew* families means the Jewish thread sewn in Babylon six hundred years before Christ's birth, remains woven into the nation's fabric.

39. Betrayal

Nothing in this world is certain except death, taxes,
and America betraying the Kurds.
JOURNALIST, JON SCHWARZ

I mentioned the Trump Administration's withdrawal of support for Kurds fighting Islamic State in 2019 was seen by most observers as a gross betrayal, given the Kurds had lost thousands on the battlefield and without them I.S's so called caliphate wouldn't have been destroyed.

But the world shouldn't have been surprised when former President Trump pulled the plug.

It seems whenever the Kurds have served America's purpose they get dumped. I guess that's because neither the US nor the regional powers want Kurdish influence to become too strong; they might begin re-asserting claims for independence, and that would never do.

Previous examples of American betrayal of her Kurdish allies go back almost a century.

The first time was in 1923 when Washington supported the Treaty of Lausanne, which allowed the British and the French to carve up Mesopotamia for themselves, but left no provision for the Kurds who'd been promised a homeland in the Treaty of Sèvres two years before.

After World War Two, America became the main colonial

power in the Middle East and supported a military coup in Iraq in 1963 which removed Abdel Karim Kassem from power. Nevertheless, Washington still cut off aid to the Kurds when a new administration was installed in Baghdad.

In the 1970s, Iraq under the leadership of Saddam Hussein had become aligned to the Soviet Union and the Nixon administration cobbled together a plan with the Shah of Iran, a US ally, to arm the Kurds in Iraq and destabilise the regime in Baghdad.

But, America didn't want to empower the Kurds enough to overthrow Saddam, because that would encourage their Kurdish cousins in Iran to try to depose the Shah. Washington just wanted Saddam weakened militarily.

So, when the Kurds had served their purpose the US supported agreements between the Shah and Saddam which included severing aid to Kurdistan. Afterwards, Saddam's forces swept into the Kurdish region and slaughtered thousands.

At the time, US Secretary of State Henry Kissinger brushed off criticism that support for the Kurds had been a cynical exercise.

He said: 'covert action should not be confused with missionary work.'

The 1980s saw a further American perfidy towards the Kurds.

Saddam's genocidal campaign in the Kurdish region had reached a peak. But, across the border, in Iran, Ayatollah Khomeini had overthrown the Shah in the Islamic Revolution of 1979 and was calling for 'Death to America'.

The US therefore supported Saddam, and even though the dictator used chemical weapons against the Kurds, the Reagan Administration opposed sanctions against Baghdad.

The Kurds were double-crossed yet again in 1991. Saddam's forces had invaded Kuwait, but were in retreat when US President George H.W. Bush called on 'the Iraqi military and Iraqi people to take matters into their own hands, to force Saddam Hussein, the dictator, to step aside'.

As a journalist I filed many stories from southern Iraq when the Shi'ites rose up in the south and from the north when the Kurds in the north rebelled and I can state, with certainty, Kurd and Shia rebel leaders were convinced the American cavalry would come riding over the hill if they took on Saddam's military might.

The opposite happened. The American military stood down and Kurdish and Shi'ite communities were massacred in their thousands.

At the time New York Times columnist Thomas Friedman explained:

Mr. Bush never supported the Kurdish and Shiite rebellions against Mr. Hussein, or for that matter any democracy movement in Iraq,' because Saddam's: 'iron fist simultaneously held Iraq together, much to the satisfaction of the American allies Turkey and Saudi Arabia.

Friedman opined that what the U.S. wanted was for the Iraqi military, not regular people, to take charge:

'Washington would have the best of all worlds: an iron-fisted Iraqi junta without Saddam Hussein, he wrote.

Images filed by journalists like me of the slaughter of Shi'ites, and Biblical scenes of Kurds fleeing to the mountains to escape massacre, didn't play well in the States and America eventually joined the British effort to establish a no-fly zone to protect the Kurds from Saddam's warplanes, but only to save face.

Then, during the Clinton Administration the post-war autonomy of the Kurds rattled Ankara's nerves because Turkey had a large Kurdish population who were also pushing for independence.

Turkey was, and still is, an important NATO ally and so the US turned a blind eye to the Turks carrying out heavy bombing raids against Kurdish PKK fighters; action which I witnessed and described in the first chapter in this book and is still continuing in north Iraq.

A further American betrayal of the Kurds occurred in 2003. The administration of George W Bush partly justified its action of invading Iraq by claiming it was to save the ethnic groups like the Kurds from persecution by Saddam's forces.

And yet, when the military campaign was over Washington still effectively gave the green light to Turkey bombing Kurdish guerrillas inside Iraq where the Turks were even allowed to establish a military base.

In all, the Kurds had been betrayed by the US eight times before Trump also turned his back on them.

40. The PKK

At the start of this book I described my first encounter with fighters of a highly active Kurdish resistance group: the PKK, but without writing about their background.

The movement was founded by Abdullah Ocalan, in 1974, as a Marxist proletarian group.

Back in the 1970s, Ocalan's original strategy was to focus on hitting Turkish military targets and ultimately overthrowing the government in Ankara. An independent Kurdish state was a secondary goal.

This contrasted sharply with the aims of, say, separatist Kurds in Iraq who've sought statehood for a hundred and twenty years, but since 2003, when Saddam Hussein was toppled, have eschewed violence as a means of achieving it.

PKK leader Ocalan had been at large when cameraman Tim and I were up in Turkey's Taurus Mountains. He was directing operations in Turkey from a sanctuary in Syria.

Six-years later, the CIA helped the Turkish secret service captured him in Kenya.

Ocalan was jailed and sentenced to death, but he escaped execution because Turkey scrapped the death penalty to help its pitch to join the European Union.

He's now aged seventy-two, and still behind bars in a prison known as 'Turkey's Alcatraz'.

Ocalan remains an inspirational figure to PKK fighters battling Islamic State and other militias in north Syria and

Turkish forces in Turkey and more recently in Iraq.

His recently revised long-term aim is to create a separate Kurdish entity with self-governing communities through local councils and parliaments; a sort of bottom up version of democracy, based on Marxist ideals.

Decades of military action needed funding and the PKK has always been bankrolled by legitimate Kurdish businesses based in Turkey, Iraq, Syria and Iran.

There's also ample evidence the movement earns millions as one the world's biggest drug cartels.

In 1993 Britain's National Intelligence Service estimated PKK coffers were swelled by US$75 million a year from narcotics trafficked in Europe alone. In 2020 the UN estimated total drug revenues amounted to US$200 annually.

Money from heroin and other hard drugs buys them Kalashnikovs, rockets, grenades, pistols, ammunition and other weaponry, which, in the early days, they sourced from former Soviet Union nations and Russia.

Nowadays the PKK buys its weapons mostly from the Czech Republic, and, according to the Turkish Government, from suppliers in the US, the UK, China, Russia, Spain and Italy.

America's policy towards the PKK is ever changing.

The Trump administration used to support Turkey's bombing of PKK bases by allowing Ankara access to a secret US unarmed drone operation out of Incirlik.

But US aerial intelligence assistance was withdrawn in response to Turkey's cross-border military incursion into Syria in late 2019.

At the same time, America firmly supported the PKK's

military wing, the YPG, as it fought against Islamic State to effectively smash the so-called caliphate and free tens of thousands from I.S's rule including Yazidis trapped on Mount Sinjar in Iraq and the citizens of Kobane, in northern Syria.

But then, the Trump administration, as we've already heard, withdrew American backing from the YPG in October 2019, leaving Kurdish families in north Syria exposed to attack from a myriad of militias roaming the region.

The Turks, meanwhile, continue their bombing of PKK bases on a regular basis using warplanes and drones.

In June 2020 President Erdogan of Turkey ordered his defence chiefs to launch Operation Claw-Tiger, the latest operation in a forty year campaign of attacks on the PKK by Turkish war planes and commandoes on the ground.

Several civilians have been killed in villages in Dohuk province and in east Kurdistan where local shepherds have lost their lives.

With the usual caveat about reliable figures from the Turkish Government, Ankara issued statistics in early 2021 showing how recruitment to the PKK had fallen to an all-time low in 2020.

There was a peak in 1983 of 1,734 new recruits, which fell to between 400 and 700 a year in the early 2000s. Recruitment peaked again in 2009 to 1,328, rocketed to an all-time high of 5,558 in 2014, but has plummeted to just fifty-two in 2020, the lowest ever.

Around 40, 000 people have died in the war between the Turkish government and the PKK, which remains a proscribed terror organisation in the US, the UK, Europe and Turkey.

41. The millennials

My fixer Karokh and I were waiting for an interviewee to show up at a shopping mall outside Erbil, late one afternoon.

The mall was the usual glitzy affair; marble floors glistened, fountains played and escalators swept up to high-end clothing shops, jewellery outlets and fast food outlets.

The glittering edifice had absolutely everything - except customers.

Some construction magnate, probably Turkish, with contacts in the Kurdish government, had built the mall halfway up a hillside, with no regard for potential customer footfall.

With no shoppers, retail staff had little choice but to stand around staring at the ceiling or trying to look busy.

I chatted to one or two of the young sales assistants. Most had perfect English, were well educated and as well informed as any other member of the Twitter/Facebook/Snapchat generation.

As I listened to their stories about how they'd graduated from university and ended up in a dead end job with no real prospects, I was struck by what was a terrible waste of young lives and brain power.

Talented Kurdish youngsters had such a big contribution to make; they were Iraqi Kurdistan's future; and yet the government had utterly failed them.

How they smartened themselves up every day to stand behind an empty counter with no customers, and yet remained so engaging and cheerful beggars belief.

I'd be chewing the carpets.

Iraq is a young country.

Nearly half Iraqi Kurdistan's six million plus population is aged under thirty.

It's a generation that's known two decades of peace, witnessed an unprecedented explosion of construction and nation building; in their minds eye they've seen the 'city on the hill,' a land their political leaders promised would be the 'new Dubai'.

Surely they're the luckiest generation in Kurdish history?

Sadly not, as a recent survey from the Kurdistan Region Statistics Office showed.

At least one in ten eighteen to thirty-four year olds are out of work and more than twenty per cent have lost hope of ever finding a job.

And it's not only because there are few jobs.

Being employed in Kurdistan is subject to a unique set of restrictions, the main one being kinship and patronage to one or other of the main political parties: the KDP and PUK.

In other words, your parents usually need to be keen supporters of one of the ruling duopoly before you even get a foot in the door of a business or government department.

It's a system that guarantees party loyalty, but it's open to abuse.

In 2014, when Iraqi Prime Minister Nouri al-Maliki decided to punish the Kurds for not handing their oil over to the Iraqi state oil company, one of the reasons he gave was the unacceptably high number of people on the Kurdish Government's payroll - around half the working population.

And Baghdad also estimated the number of people receiving

a Government salary without doing any work at all, had passed the one million mark.

Small wonder there's a Kurdish joke which goes:

Passenger to taxi driver: 'I'm so poor I have to work two more jobs, as well as my work for the government.'

Taxi driver to passenger: 'So, when do you sleep?'

Passenger to taxi driver: 'At my government job.'

Young Kurdish women have a particularly tough time of it in the jobs market.

In 2020 seventy per cent of females under twenty four were out of work and thirty-six per cent of women aged twenty five to thirty four had no job.

Social norms are partly to blame.

A World Bank report in 2019 found mixing with men, harassment, and long working hours were deterrents and barriers. Another drawback was women who finished maternity leave weren't legally guaranteed their jobs back.

Women can earn more in the private sector than in a government job but they expected to work in retail or hospitality.

So those who don't cherish standing in a shopping mall selling cosmetics or a hotel reception desk, inevitably end up working for the Government in poorly paid health and education jobs.

One young lady told me, 'My brother sanctions my choice of employment, he doesn't allow me to take any job in the private sector.'

Another said, 'I want to work in the building industry, but my father would never approve of that.'

Kurdistan's universities - fifteen public and two private - are currently turning out 6,000 graduates a year into the stagnant jobs market, where would-be doctors, lawyers and the like are often forced into taking unskilled jobs because they can't find work.

A Deputy Prime Minister sparked anger in 2019 by saying, 'Graduates shouldn't shun menial jobs like digging roads.'

He tweeted: 'It is normal for graduates not to immediately find a job in their field and there is no shame in taking an opportunity that is unrelated to one's program of study.'

That's a hard pill to swallow for someone who's studied medicine for seven years.

There are jobs in the private sector for students and school leavers, but legions of employers ignore minimum wage rules. Some factory workers earn just over US$10 a day for a ten-hour day, six days a week.

No employment means no income and without money Kurdish youngsters can't get married, start a family or support one.

This is in a society where the only socially recognised scenario for sexual relations is marriage.

Small wonder a generation of young Kurds feel they're trapped as singletons.

42. They reap what they sow

Stagnation is the main challenge facing 'Generation 2000', made manifest in the absence of viable prospects and opportunities for major social and economic milestones that leaves this group socially and economically excluded. Many of them are manipulated by a range of opportunists, such as armed non-state actors, sectarian entrepreneurs and smugglers, seeking to exploit the existing social and political dynamics while promising something more.

SHIVAN FAZIL, UNIVERSITY OF LONDON'S SCHOOL OF ORIENTAL AND AFRICAN STUDIES, IN SEPTEMBER 2018,

Signs of frustration and general disillusionment amongst the young of Kurdistan have already manifested themselves.

In September 2017, Kurdistan's independence referendum was largely boycotted by young Kurds, who said they had no time for the old guard of political leaders.

When asked why the new generation was so reluctant to vote, a female interviewee responded: 'Young people saw the vote as legitimising the rule of the old political class and therefore their continuation'.

Another said: 'The youth saw the referendum as serving the interests of the old rulers.'

Three months after the referendum boycott, a youth-led protest erupted in Sulaimaniyah province.

After years of corruption, nepotism and unpaid salaries, young Kurds torched cars and government offices and called on the administration in Erbil to step down.

The crackdown was swift. Tanks appeared on the streets and at least five protesters were shot dead.

Early in 2018 young people took to the streets again in Sulaymaniyah, Erbil and Dohuk in an unprecedented wave of protests against salary cuts. Teachers, students and health professionals staged a week-long strike.

And when the polling booths opened in Iraq's parliamentary election in May 2018, highly disillusioned Kurdish millennials stayed away again- the overall turnout was only forty four per cent.

That feeling of dissatisfaction with the political leadership still exists. A 2019 poll of Kurds aged fifteen to twenty nine found that thirty five percent saw emigration to Europe as a solution to their lack of job prospects and a better life.

If young people continue to leave, they'd follow generations of others.

In the summer of 2015, thousands of millennials paid people smugglers to spirit them into Greece and Turkey where they joined Syrian refugees on their way to Europe.

The Kurdish Government's Ministry of Health reported that between 2014 and 2018, 1400 newly qualified doctors left for good for new posts overseas.

Meanwhile, Iraq's Federation of Refugees estimates at least three hundred young Kurds leave for a new life in another country every day, representing a shocking brain drain of youthful talent.

What I found most worrying is that disillusioned young

men with no job prospects can potentially be seduced into the murderous jihadi groups like Islamic State either by radical Kurdish clerics or by on line groomers.

Their message to disaffected Kurdish youth, 'your own corrupt government has let you down, so fight it.'

That's a siren call that will resonate easily with some young men out there.

43. Saving the economy

In early to mid 2020, falling oil prices, and the impact of the COVID-19 virus, meant the regime in Erbil had effectively slid into bankruptcy, meanwhile protests against government corruption and mismanagement continued.

In one protest farmers dumped tons of unsold tomatoes on a highway near Erbil to show their anger over the government's poor handling of Kurdistan's agricultural industry. More protests were planned.

The government in Baghdad wasn't in much better shape. Prime Minister, Mustafa Al-Khadimi, who'd been given the nod by Teheran and Washington, pledged to fight corruption, but low world oil prices had a massive impact on the economy. The COVID-19 virus also took its human and economic toll. By October 2020 Kurdistan had 1,000 COVID cases a day.

Getting Erbil and Baghdad's economies back on track was vital not only for both governments, but Iraq's financial stability had been also one of the keys to an American troop drawdown.

Washington dusted off an idea the Obama State Department set in motion in December 2014 which involved the two Iraqi governments working together for the common good.

The proposal to take Baghdad and Erbil out of bankruptcy went like this:

The Kurds control some of Iraq's most valuable crude and the Kurdish Government (KEG) should increase its oil production from about 450,000 barrels a day to one million.

Iraq's State Organisation for Marketing of Oil (SOMO) would market and sell about four-fifths of that output and the KRG would keep about 200,000 barrels to meet its existing oil sales commitments.

SOMO would blend the Kurd's higher-grade crude with Iraq's more ordinary oil, creating an expected increase of US$5 per barrel in the price Iraq commands for its exports. The two would benefit from a revenue share from the ensuing sales.

Meanwhile, the KRG would approve as many new oil drilling areas in its vast untapped fields as possible, to ramp up production and U.S. and international oil firms would assist in increasing drilling and production as quickly as possible.

U.S. and Iraqi security forces would join Kurdish forces in ensuring the safety of drilling sites, supply lines, and pipelines to keep oil flowing.

The KRG would maintain the contractual relationships with international oil partners, while SOMO would market the new blend.

SOMO will pay international partners their monthly dues owed under existing contracts and keep the rest of the sale proceeds, sharing seventeen per cent of the Iraq budget with the Kurds.

Iraq would in turn stay its legal claims over KRG oil issues.

If all the above was put into practice the potential impact to Iraq's treasury was estimated at $15 billion annually, which it would share with the Kurds.

That's was the plan. At the time of writing Washington was still waiting for Baghdad and Erbil to implement it.

44. Not in the news

Each month the Washington Kurdistan Institute sends me a summary of news events affecting Kurdish communities across Iran, Iraq, Turkey and Syria.

Mainstream media wouldn't cover any of the stories.

To redress lack of reportage I summarise January 2021's edition, which is a typical month and I hope an invaluable insight of what Kurdish people suffer on a daily basis.

IRAN: Iran's crackdown on Kurdish political activity continued into 2021 with Piranshahr's Islamic Revolutionary Court sentencing two Kurdish men, Omar Khagezada and Abbas Sadiqi, to five years in prison for 'cooperation with a Kurdish opposition party'.

The same court sentenced a former member of the Democratic Party of Iranian Kurdistan, Sobhan Ahmadi, to one year in prison in Saqqez. Concurrently, Iranian security forces arrested a Kurdish labour activist named Jawanmier Muradi in Kermanshah.

Muradi was previously imprisoned several times for activism and participation in anti-government protests.

The Kurdistan Human Rights Association reported Iranian authorities arrested five Kurds in Baneh, four of whom were identified as Ayoub Sadqi, Zahir Khudaie, Mohammed Karimi, and Basid Jamal.

Lastly, the Hengaw Organisation for Human Rights claimed the Iranian regime detained 437 Kurdish activists, including minors, in 2020.

Tehran's Islamic Revolutionary Court sentenced the secretary of the Iranian Writers' Association, Arash Ganji, to eleven years in prison on charges that included 'spreading anti-government propaganda'.

Ganji was initially put on trial for translating a book about the Kurdish revolution in Syria while imprisoned.

PEN America condemned the verdict and described it as an 'absurd and unquestionable violation of the fundamental human right to free expression'.

Four Kurdish border porters (Kolbars) suffered injuries last week. A Kolbar named Daniel Darzian was injured when he fell from a cliff near Hawraman, and Iranian border guards shot and wounded two Kolbars in Nowsud: Paiam Sohrabi and Abdul Karim.

Iranian authorities wounded a third Kolbar in Salas-e Babajani.

Fifty-nine Kolbars were killed, and at least 179 were injured in 2020, mostly at the hands of the Iranian regime.

IRAQ: The Kurdistan Regional Government and Government of Iraq finally reached an agreement regarding Iraq's 2021 budget. The agreement, which was announced by the head of the KRG delegation, Deputy Prime Minister of the Kurdistan Region Qubad Talabani, entails the KRG's provision of revenue from the sale of 250,000 barrels of oil per day and fifty per cent of income from border crossings to the Government of Iraq in exchange for its share of the federal budget.

The Council of Representatives of Iraq is set to hold the first reading of the 2021 budget bill despite lingering doubts regarding its likelihood of passage over objections from

Iranian-backed Shia parties.

Many of Iraq's Iranian-backed Members of Parliament have criticised the bill's proposed spending, distribution of funds to Iraq's southern provinces, and agreement with the KRG, which remains opposed by Iranian-backed parties.

Two Kurdish security forces were injured by an explosion while removing a booby-trapped ISIS flag in Sulaymaniyah Governorate's Said Sadiq District.

Three Iraqi Army members, including an officer, were killed by a Da'esh IED in Kirkuk Governorate's Haweja District.

ISIS also attacked Iraqi Army personnel in Diyala Governorate's Jawala, killing one and wounding seven.

ISIS continues to exploit the fragile security situation in Iraq's 'Disputed Territories' that was exacerbated when Iraqi forces and Iranian-backed militias expelled the Peshmerga on October 16, 2017.

SYRIA: The Turkish military and its proxies continued to launch indirect fire attacks on Ain Essa and its suburbs.

The Syrian Democratic Forces repelled several attacks in the area, which has remained under de facto Russian control since the October 2019 US withdrawal.

Kurdish officials have accused Russia of failing to oppose ongoing Turkish attacks intended to divide the Kurdish region and disconnect it from Kurdish towns like Kobani in a manner that would make the region ripe for invasion by Turkey and/ or the Assad regime.

Turkey has already established a military outpost near the strategic M4 Motorway.

Meanwhile, the President of the Executive Committee of the Syrian Democratic Council Ilham Ahmad has called for

Russia to support the self-administration and said she held them accountable for bearing 'the mistakes of the Syrian government, greatly'.

TURKEY: The Turkish government, despite several calls from European nations and a ruling from the European Convention on Human Rights has refused to release the jailed former head of the Peoples' Democratic Party Selahattin Demirtas.

Turkish President Recep Tayyip Erdogan blasted the ECHR's ruling, and an Ankara court claimed it dismissed the ruling, which was presented by Demirtas's lawyers, because it was not issued in the Turkish language.

The Turkish government has arrested more Kurds and HDP members, including two refugees from Kobani, in its ongoing campaign against Kurdish political activity.

Ankara's chief prosecutor summited indictments against 108 Kurdish politicians for participation in the October 2014 Kobani protests.

Münir Karaloğlu, the government trustee who replaced the elected Kurdish mayor of Diyarbakir, has fired eighty-four public sector employees.

The Turkish government has now removed sixty of sixty five Kurdish mayors who were elected in the 2019 elections.

At the same time, the HDP office in Bursa Province's Inegöl District was set on fire in what appears to be the latest in a string of hate crimes that have targeted Turkey's Kurdish population.

Kurdish political prisoners protesting the Turkish government's ongoing isolation of imprisoned Kurdish leader Abdullah Ocalan continued their hunger strike for the second month in a row.

Turkey's political prisoners have previously used hunger strikes to draw attention to the Turkish government's discriminatory policies, authoritarianism, and imposition of a visitation ban on Ocalan.

45. Final thoughts

Will the Kurds be able to establish their own independent state in the twenty-first century? And will Iraqi Kurdistan become a fully-fledged nation recognised by the international community?

In my view they have as much chance as the Palestinians, so the answer has to be: no - at least, not in my lifetime.

I'm sure many Kurds will disagree with them, but here are the final thoughts of a humble correspondent who's been reporting and working in Iraq, on and off, for decades.

Kurdish nationalist groups lack unity of purpose. For example, as we've seen, the Turkey based PKK, has no meaningful connections with Komola in Iran, other than sharing the same Marxist goals.

And even if Kurdish factions were united, Iraq, Iran, Syria and Turkey will never voluntarily cede swathes of their own territory to allow the Kurds to form a separate independent state.

Narrowing the same question to Iraqi Kurdistan, where the population of over six million voted by a huge majority for independence in September 2017, no regional power supports their full autonomy, except arguably Israel, but even that's in principle only.

Meanwhile, America and her Western allies, including Britain, France and Germany, are firmly against a breakaway northern Iraq. They support a united federal Iraq especially as the country as a whole remains so fragile, politically and economically.

But, even if the major powers swallowed the argument Iraqi Kurdistan was stable and deserved independence Western governments would insist on the scrapping of tribal politics, and that's never going to happen.

Tribalism is part of the make-up of Kurdistan. It raged a hundred years ago when officials like Gertrude Bell reported back to London that Kurdish chiefs were constantly fighting each other.

From time to time they still do in the modern age.

As recently as the mid 1990s the ruling KDP and PUK parties waged a futile and destructive civil war.

Relations have improved, but at the time of writing, in early 2021, the KDP and PUK enjoy only a cordial alliance, rather than a brotherly partnership.

As far as a true democratic system goes, the two ruling parties don't regard political competition as healthy and welcome. Far from it.

Earlier in this book we heard how the Gorran party's Dr Shayan Askeri suffered death threats when she challenged endemic corruption in the political set up and there are many more credible reports of citizens being investigated and detained when they're suspected of favouring opposition candidates.

Dutch journalist Judit Neurink wrote about the scale of intimidation in May 2020. She said: 'I have seen TV studios set on fire and journalists beaten, harassed and arrested. Independent papers have now disappeared from the streets, and are now fighting for survival online.

The freedoms the Kurds had worked so hard to prioritise, have been taken away by politicians who always put their own survival first.

Kurdistan's rulers only know one way to react: oppressing the people and setting them against one another. The divide between the PUK and KDP is wider than ever, with fears of the region splitting the region in two.'

But let's set all the above to one side for a moment and fantasise that world powers agreed the Kurds had a strong case for independence, the KDP and PUK decided they could work together and accepted a truly democratic political system, then the next question would be: how could landlocked, independent Iraqi Kurdistan survive on its own when its economy is oil dependent?

The answer is it can't, and the evidence is there already.

Kurdish oil exports peaked at around 600,000 barrels a day in 2016, and have been in decline since, partly because the Kurds' single export pipeline to Turkey is regularly bombed by groups like Islamic State and the PKK, or broken into by oil smugglers. The Turks also shut the pipeline down when they're carrying out military raids against PKK guerrillas.

To add to the Kurds' woes world oil prices collapsed in the spring of 2020 and Erbil's long running dispute with central government in Baghdad over sharing oil revenues rumbled on, leaving Kurdish government debt standing at a whopping $27 billion.

With oil revenues at only US$30 million a month it meant one point two million Kurds on the government payroll wait months for their pay cheques; this as living standards rise and expectations rise faster, with families yearning for politicians to make good on promises of electricity, clean water, better health and educational facilities and access to employment.

The reality is an independent Kurdistan reliant only on oil

revenues is a busted flush. It just can't work.

Even though Kurdish millennials live in a land of broken dreams run by a politically and financially bankrupt government, I need to end this book about the indomitable Kurds on a positive note.

Foreign visitors like me are constantly surprised by lively, dynamic cities like Dohuk, Erbil and Sulaimaniyah, with their skyscrapers, lushly landscaped parks, a state-of-the-airport, bustling shopping malls and high-rise apartment blocks.

This is what the strong Kurdish spirit, good security and years of income from oil can achieve.

Iraqi Kurdistan is also stunningly beautiful; cities and towns can match any in Europe in terms of infrastructure, culture and entertainment. Its people are welcoming to most foreigners.

When I got into conversation with young Kurds, I found they were find a generation, which looked forwards, not backwards to their parents' and grandparents' world of persecution and betrayal.

They're educated, they've embraced social media as much as any young generation in the West and as long as the brightest and the best remain in Kurdistan, and not be scattered to the ends of the Earth, then Iraqi Kurdistan will continue on the same trajectory, not as an independent nation - that can never work -but as a shining beacon of enterprise and human triumph over adversity.

The youth of Kurdistan have a limitless potential that deserves to flourish and thrive.

I pray they remain in their homeland to achieve their dreams.